WRITE IT ANYWAY

HOW TO TURN YOUR HEALING STORY INTO A SELF PUBLISHED BOOK THAT HELPS OTHERS

CAROLINE BAKKER

Write it Anyway: How to Turn Your Healing Story Into a Self Published Book That Helps Others

ISBN: 979-8-89860-415-8

Cover Design and Interior Layout by: Caroline Bakker

Disclaimer: This book is for informational purposes only. It is not intended to replace professional medical, psychological, or financial advice. The author and publisher disclaim responsibility for any adverse effects or consequences resulting from the use of information contained herein. Readers should consult appropriate professionals before making decisions related to health, wellness, or other matters discussed in this book.

Edition: First Edition, Launched 22 November 2025
Version: 28 October 2025

For permissions or inquiries, contact: publisher@carolinebakker.com
Contact information: https://www.carolinebakker.com/

Connect & Share

If this book moves you, I'd
love to see it in your hands.

Share your favourite pages
or moments and tag me on
Instagram:

@amazonwarriorau

Your stories inspire others to begin
their healing journey.

DEDICATION

For every soul who writes to remember.

For every being who has ever doubted their voice,

silenced their truth, or waited for permission.

For the ones who carry stories in their bones—

the quiet, the brave, the tender, and the strong.

And for every story that was never told—

may this book be your nudge to begin.

A NOTE ON DIVINE TIMING

THE ENERGY BEHIND WRITE IT ANYWAY

The birth of *Write It Anyway* wasn't random — it was aligned with divine timing and intention.

Its global release date, **22 November**, carries a powerful numerological vibration. In numerology, **22** is known as a *Master Number* — the **Master Builder**. It represents manifestation, creation, and the ability to turn dreams into tangible form. This book, too, is about doing exactly that: transforming your pain, wisdom, and healing into art that lives beyond you.

When you look even deeper, the ISBN — **979-8-89860-415-8** — also holds meaning.

If you add the digits together (9 + 7 + 9 + 8 + 8 + 9 + 8 + 6 + 0 + 4 + 1 + 5 + 8 = 82 → 8 + 2 = 10 → 1 + 0 = **1**), the number reduces to **1** — the vibration of *new beginnings, leadership, and creation*.

Combined, **22** (the Master Builder) and **1** (the Creator) reflect the essence of this book: building something meaningful from the raw material of your life.

Nothing about this project was accidental. Every choice — from the launch date to the numbers printed on its spine — was guided by alignment, intuition, and faith in divine order.

This book isn't just about writing — it's about remembering that everything in life, including your story, unfolds in perfect timing.

READER'S KEY TERMS

A SIMPLE GUIDE TO HELP YOU UNDERSTAND THE LANGUAGE AND ENERGY OF THIS BOOK.

A

AI Co-Creation — Using artificial intelligence tools, such as ChatGPT, to support your writing process through brainstorming, structure, or editing—while maintaining your authentic voice.

Authentic Voice — The tone and truth that emerge when you write from your heart rather than performance or perfectionism.

B

Body-Based Writing (Embodied Writing) — Writing that connects your physical sensations, emotions, and intuition to your creative process for deeper authenticity.

Brand Story — The message, mission, and emotional core of who you are as an author; how your personal journey connects to your reader.

Burnout — A state of emotional, mental, and physical depletion caused by overworking or self-neglect; often healed through rest, boundaries, and self-compassion.

C

Cycle Syncing — Aligning your creative rhythm and self-care with the hormonal phases of your menstrual cycle to optimize energy and focus.

D

Drafting — The initial stage of writing where ideas flow freely without judgment or editing.

E

Editing — The process of refining your manuscript for clarity, flow, and emotional integrity while preserving your original essence.

Emotional Reparenting — Meeting the unmet needs of your younger self through compassion and understanding; often part of the healing that arises through writing.

Energetic Hygiene — The practice of clearing emotional residue through grounding, journaling, or mindful movement to stay energetically balanced while writing.

Embodied Writing — (See *Body-Based Writing.*)

Expressive Writing — A therapeutic writing practice developed by Dr. James Pennebaker, focusing on emotional truth to support healing and insight.

F

Flow State — A creative zone where focus, energy, and inspiration align; time feels suspended and writing feels effortless.

H

Healing Book — A blend of memoir and self-help written to turn personal experiences into wisdom that helps others heal.

Healing Through Story — The act of transforming pain into purpose by writing about your experiences with meaning and awareness.

Healing Voice — The calm, integrated tone that emerges once you've processed your pain and can write from understanding rather than raw emotion.

I

Integration — The process of embodying the lessons, insights, and emotional healing that occur through writing.

Inner Editor — The critical inner voice that can block creativity during early drafts; learning to quiet it allows authentic expression to emerge.

L

Lived Experience — Real-life moments and challenges that shape your personal story and form the foundation of your healing message.

M

Memoir — A narrative style that tells your true story through a personal, emotional lens; used as a foundation for healing books.

Mind-Body Connection — The awareness that thoughts, emotions, and body sensations are interconnected and influence creativity and well-being.

N

Nervous System Regulation — The practice of calming and

balancing your body's stress response to maintain clarity, creativity, and emotional safety while writing.

P

Perfectionism — The belief that your work must be flawless before it's shared; a creative block often rooted in fear of rejection or visibility.

Proof Copy — A printed test version of your book used to review formatting, design, and feel before publication.

Publishing Roadmap — A structured plan that outlines the steps from draft to publication, including editing, design, and marketing.

R

Restorative Creativity — Writing or creating in a way that nourishes your energy instead of draining it.

Ritual (Writing Ritual) — A simple, sacred routine that signals your body and mind it's time to write—such as lighting a candle, journaling, or taking deep breaths.

S

Self-Compassion — Treating yourself with kindness and understanding, especially during self-doubt or creative struggle.

Self-Publishing — Releasing your book independently using platforms like Amazon KDP or IngramSpark, giving you full control and ownership.

Sensitivity — Emotional awareness that can be both a gift and a challenge for healing writers; used consciously, it deepens empathy and authenticity.

Story Medicine — The idea that stories have the power to heal both writer and reader by offering connection, validation, and meaning.

T

Trauma-Informed Writing — Writing with sensitivity to emotional triggers, creating safety for both the author and reader.

Traditional Publishing — Publishing through a professional company that handles editing, marketing, and distribution in exchange for royalties and rights.

V

Visibility — The act of being seen for your work; reframed in this book as a practice of courage and service rather than self-promotion.

Voice (Author Voice) — The unique rhythm, language, and emotional tone that make your writing unmistakably yours.

CONTENTS

PREFACE

THE UNIVERSE ALWAYS SENDS WHAT YOU'RE READY FOR

It was well past my bedtime, but I couldn't sleep. My mind was still alive with energy — the kind that hums quietly after something important has shifted. Earlier that evening, I had stood on stage at the Sharjah Children's Book Festival — **my first official speaking engagement**, and my first time ever standing on a stage like that. I'd been invited by *IngramSpark* to join a panel alongside authors and self-publishers, but nothing could have prepared me for how it would feel to be up there — lights warm on my skin, heart pounding, words flowing.

I had walked in thinking I'd simply share some lessons about self-publishing — a few tips, some encouragement, maybe a story or two. **But what unfolded went much deeper.** As I began to speak about my journey — writing through depression, burnout, ADHD, PMDD (severe PMS), and motherhood — something in the room shifted. Faces softened.

People leaned forward. There was this unspoken recognition that writing isn't just about creating — it's about healing.

When the panel ended, people came up to me, eyes bright, sharing pieces of their own stories. One woman said quietly,

> *"You made me believe I can actually do it. I can write my story."*

That stayed with me. Driving home that night through the busy streets of Sharjah, I replayed the day over and over in my mind. It wasn't the public speaking itself that lit me up — it was the connection. For the first time in a long time, **I felt aligned.** I realised I didn't just love writing books; I loved sharing my story. I loved seeing people remember their own power through words.

During that event I met a woman I now believe I was **destined** to meet — a soul sister, a divine connection. The moment **Yasmen Ahmed**, author of *Lies That Shaped You*, walked into the room with her radiant smile and grounded presence, I felt it: that quiet recognition, like a universal remembering. She was a mama too, and from our very first conversation, I knew we were meant to cross paths. There was no small talk, just ease — the kind that happens when two people are on the same wavelength of purpose and growth.

We exchanged numbers that day, and we've been in contact almost daily ever since. We get on like a house on fire — swapping voice notes, cheering each other on, holding space for the big dreams and the messy moments. She's been quietly encouraging me from the sidelines, reflecting my power back to me, reminding me who I am when I forget, and gently expanding my vision of what's possible.

Through Yasmen, I discovered books that cracked me open again — *The Magic of Thinking Big* by David Schwartz, *Big Magic* by Elizabeth Gilbert, and *Rich as Fck** by Amanda Frances. Those books reawakened something in me: the dreamer, the visionary, the future self I had buried beneath exhaustion and responsibility.

I began refining my goals and leaning back into manifestation — not as a performance, but as a practice of remembrance. I read *The Having* by Suh Yoon Lee and began anchoring into deep, cellular gratitude — not just for what I wanted to call in, but for what was already here.

I even recorded a Future Self audio in my own voice, describing the woman I was becoming before she arrived — the one who rests without guilt, leads with rhythm, speaks with conviction, and loves with her whole heart. I listened to it every night before bed, and I believe it helped me realign my timeline — not by bypassing the work, but by meeting the version of me who had already done the healing. That was the spark that brought this book to life.

This book is for the souls who have lived many lives in one body. For the storytellers who are afraid no one will care. For the creators who carry sacred stories but don't know where to begin. And for the souls who know they're here to help — but just need a nudge.

If you're holding this book, consider this your nudge.

I wrote *Write It Anyway* because you don't need to be perfect to begin. You just need to be honest. You need to believe that your story — with all its chaos, pauses, and rebirths — is worth telling. Because it is.

Whether you're holding a half-finished manuscript, an idea scribbled on a napkin, or just a quiet feeling in your chest that you're meant to write something — this is your sign.

Because someone out there is waiting for your words.

Write it anyway.

PART ONE
INTRODUCTION
THE POWER OF WRITING AS HEALING

WRITING AS REMEMBERING

YOUR STORY IS MEDICINE

WRITING AS REMEMBERING

For most of my life, writing was something I did in the in-between moments — the late nights, the quiet mornings, the times when life felt too heavy to carry alone. I never set out to be an author. I set out to understand myself.

My first real pieces of writing weren't essays or manuscripts; they were survival notes. Journal pages filled with confusion, longing, hope, and prayer. I didn't realise it then, but every sentence I wrote was stitching together parts of me I had lost along the way — the brave parts, the soft parts, the ones that still believed in possibility.

Writing became my way home.

When I finally began sharing those words — in blog posts, meditations, social media captions — people began to respond. They'd say, *"You put into words what I've always felt but never knew how to say."* And that was when I realised something profound: the more honest I was, the more universal my story became. The moments I was most afraid to share were often the ones that connected most deeply. **That's the heartbeat of this book**.

> **It's about remembering the voice you silenced to survive. It's about reclaiming your truth after years of performing, pleasing, and pretending**

- Caroline Bakker

Write It Anyway isn't just about writing a book. It's about **remembering** the voice you silenced to survive. It's about **reclaiming** your truth after years of performing, pleasing, and pretending. It's about creating space for the stories that ache to be told — not because they're polished, but because they're real.

The act of writing has always been sacred to me. It's a bridge between who we've been and who we're becoming. When you write with honesty, you begin to integrate the parts of yourself that once felt fragmented. You start to see the pattern behind the pain. You start to witness yourself — fully, compassionately, without judgement.

I believe every soul has a story inside them that could change a life — sometimes her own, sometimes someone else's. And yet, so many never tell it. We get caught up in the noise: *Who am I to write a book? What if no one reads it? What if I'm not good enough?* I've asked myself those same questions.

But here's the truth: **you don't need permission**. You don't need credentials. You don't even need confidence. You just need to begin — with one sentence, one page, one small act of courage at a time.

This book will guide you through that process — not as a manual, but as a companion. You'll find stories from my own journey of writing and healing, as well as practical steps to help you shape your story, self-publish with confidence, and most importantly, stay connected to your "why."

> *Because writing a book isn't just about getting published. It's about getting honest. It's about showing up to your life with open hands and saying, I'm ready to see what's really here.*

Throughout these pages, you'll learn to write from the body, not just the mind. To trust your intuition as much as your outline. To hold your story with reverence — even the chapters you once wanted to hide. **You'll learn how to *write as a practice of healing, not perfection.***

If you're reading this, you already feel the call. There's a story in you that refuses to stay silent any longer. You can feel it — that quiet hum in your chest, the tug to put words to what you've lived through.

So this is your invitation. To write the book you've been carrying inside you. To tell the truth you've been afraid to speak.

To trust that your words matter — not because they're flawless, but because they're yours.

Write it anyway. Because you never know who will find themselves in your story — and maybe, through your courage, begin to write their own.

ACTING LIKE AN AUTHOR
BEFORE I BELIEVED I WAS

Before I ever called myself a writer, I was already acting like one. I just didn't know it yet. I was the woman scribbling ideas in the notes app while waiting in line. The one who stayed up too late reworking a sentence no one would ever see. The one who carried a pen in every bag "just in case." Writing was always there — quietly anchoring me through every season of becoming.

But for years, I didn't let myself *own* it.

I told myself I wasn't a "real" writer because I didn't have a book deal, or an agent, or a perfectly organised writing routine. I had a busy life, a young child, a brain that worked differently, and a thousand excuses. I kept waiting for some external validation to make it official — a title, a paycheck, a moment where someone else would say, *Now you're ready.* **But that moment never came**.

What did come were tiny, persistent whispers — the kind that show up when you're doing dishes, walking the dog, or lying awake at 2 a.m. They said, *Just write it.* Not because it's perfect. Not because you're ready. But because you need to.

And that's when something in me shifted.

> **It's about embodiment — living in alignment with the version of you who already exists in potential. It's about showing up as if it's already true, until it becomes true.**

- Caroline Bakker

I realised that "acting like an author" isn't about pretending or performing. It's about embodiment — living in alignment with the version of you who already exists in potential. It's about showing up *as if* it's already true, until it becomes true.

That's the paradox of creation: **you become the thing by doing it before you believe you are it**.

When I look back, I can see how this truth has threaded itself through my whole life. Long before I knew about the Law of Assumption or the Law of Attraction, I was living them — intuitively, instinctively.

I remember being in high school when there was a ski trip that only a handful of students would be selected for. I wanted to go more than anything. The odds weren't in my favour — dozens of students applied, and only a few spots were available — but I didn't let that stop me. I imagined myself there, felt what it would be like to be chosen, and wrote a letter that came straight from the heart. I still remember the thrill when my name appeared on the final list. It wasn't luck. It was alignment.

Years later, during my studies at Inholland University in Amsterdam, another opportunity came up — a volunteer project in Indonesia, limited to just twenty students. Again, I poured myself into the application, visualised being there, and trusted that if it was meant for me, it would be mine. And it was. That trip changed everything.

Looking back, those moments weren't about luck or privilege. They were early lessons in creative embodiment — in becoming before becoming. I didn't have the words for it then, but I was already living the energy of "write it anyway."

That same energy guided me when I began self-publishing. I had no idea what I was doing, no credentials, no guarantee anyone would read a word. But I acted like an author — and eventually, I became one.

The thing is, waiting for permission will keep you stuck forever. The mind will always find reasons why you're not ready — not educated enough, not experienced enough, not polished enough. But the soul doesn't care about that. The soul only cares that you begin.

When you act as if you already are the writer you're becoming, something powerful happens. The Universe starts rearranging itself around your belief. Opportunities begin to show up. Ideas land. People appear. You start to *see* yourself differently — not as someone trying, but as someone becoming.

> **The moment you decide to believe in the possibility of your dream, the Universe begins to rearrange itself to make it real.**
>
> - Caroline Bakker

And the truth is, that energy — the quiet, steady decision to start before you feel ready — is what will carry you through every stage of this journey. Because writing isn't about waiting for confidence. It's about writing your way into it.

So if you're reading this, and that familiar voice is whispering that you're not ready, here's your reminder: you don't need to be ready. You just need to be willing.

Start showing up like the author you already are. Make time to write, even when no one's watching. Treat your ideas with respect, even if they feel small. Create before you feel qualified.

Speak about your book in the present tense. Because when you start embodying the version of you who's already written it — you collapse the distance between dream and reality.

Every author you've ever admired started this way. They began by *acting like it was already possible.* **And maybe, just maybe, that's what brought you to this page too.**

PRACTICE: EMBODYING THE AUTHOR WITHIN

Take a moment to slow down. Breathe. Feel your feet on the ground.

Now, imagine the version of you who has already written the book that lives inside your heart.

See yourself — the way you sit, speak, move, and hold herself.

Notice how your energy feels — grounded, calm, quietly confident.

You're not trying to prove anything anymore. You are simply being who you already knew you could become.

This is your Future Self — and this version already exists.

You don't have to wait until your book is finished to meet yourself. You can start showing up as yourself *today*.

Grab your journal and answer these prompts:

1 Who is the version of me that has already written my book?

Describe their energy, environment, habits, priorities.

2 What do you believe about yourself and your purpose?

What stories have you stopped telling herself about why you aren't ready?

3 How do you begin your day? How do you treat your creative work?

What boundaries do you hold? What rituals ground you before you writes?

4 What small action can I take this week to begin embodying that energy?

It could be as simple as writing for fifteen minutes, sharing one truth online, or introducing yourself as an author the next time someone asks what you do.

5 What fears still hold me back from claiming my identity as a writer?

Write them down. Let them be seen. Then, beneath each one, write:

And I'm doing it anyway.

Remember:

You don't become an author the day your book is published.

You become an author the day you decide to start acting like one.

And this — this moment right now, with your hand on your heart and your pen moving across the page — is where that decision begins.

MY STORY: WRITING AS HEALING

I f you've ever wondered how someone becomes a writer, I'll tell you the truth: it doesn't happen all at once. It happens in fragments — in moments when life cracks you open and you're left searching for language that can hold the weight of it all.

My story didn't begin in a publishing house or a creative writing class. It began in the quiet corners of my life — in the journals I filled when I couldn't sleep, in the voice memos I recorded between tears, in the words I never planned to share. Writing was never a career goal. It was survival.

When I started writing, I was unraveling.

Motherhood had stretched me thin, burnout had hollowed me out, and the combination of ADHD and PMDD (severe PMS) made even the simplest days feel like uphill climbs. I had spent years pushing through — through exhaustion, through grief, through the invisible expectations of being "fine." But my body had other plans. My mind was scattered, my nervous system was drained, and I had forgotten what rest felt like.

That's when I began to write. Not for an audience, not for likes or validation — just for me. I wrote because it was the only place I could be honest.

At first, it was messy. Angry. Raw. But slowly, something shifted. The words began to soften. They started to sound less like survival, and more like remembering — remembering who I was before the burnout, before the noise, before the world told me who to be.

Each page became a mirror. A confession. A homecoming.

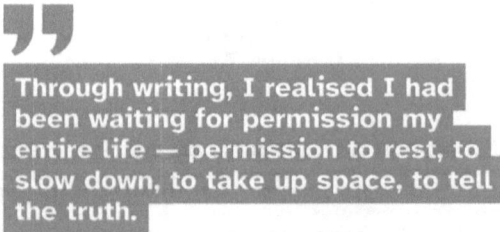

Through writing, I realised I had been waiting for permission my entire life — permission to rest, to slow down, to take up space, to tell the truth.

- Caroline Bakker

Through writing, I realised I had been waiting for permission my entire life — permission to rest, to slow down, to take up space, to tell the truth. The page gave me that permission. It didn't judge me for changing my mind. It didn't interrupt or fix me. It simply held me.

And somewhere along the way, that practice of self-expression became my **medicine**. It wasn't about writing the perfect story. It was about *becoming whole again*.

When I started sharing small pieces of my story online — first through blog posts, later through guided meditations and essays — something unexpected happened. People began to write back. They said things like, *"I thought I was the only one who felt like this."*

Those words reminded me why storytelling matters. Because every time one of us tells the truth, someone else feels less alone. **That's when I began to see writing not just as therapy, but as purpose**.

Each chapter of my life — the burnout, the healing, the late ADHD diagnosis, the rebuilding — became part of a bigger narrative. I wasn't just recovering; I was transforming. And that transformation was asking to be shared.

So I kept writing. Even on the days when the words wouldn't come. Even when my hands shook as I pressed "publish." Even when the old voices whispered, *Who do you think you are?* Because each time I wrote, I came closer to myself.

Now, looking back, I can see that writing didn't just heal me — it remade me. It helped me integrate the parts I used to hide, the ones that didn't fit neatly into a perfect image. It gave me back my voice — not the one that performs, but the one that *feels*.

That's what this book is about. Not just how to write, but how to live as a writer — awake, open, and anchored in truth. Because when you learn to write from your heart, you're not just creating art. You're creating alignment. **You're telling your soul:** *I'm listening now.*

WHAT THIS BOOK CAN (AND CAN'T) DO

Before we go any further, I want to set the tone for the journey ahead. This book is a framework — a conversation, an invitation, a companion on your creative path. It's here to awaken something in you, **not replace your intuition**.

What This Book *Can* Do:

- Help you remember why your story matters.
- Teach you to write with honesty that heals, not perfection that hides.
- Offer the mindset, structure, and support to finally finish your book.
- Guide you to self-publish and share your work from a place of purpose, not pressure.
- Remind you that you're not behind — you're right on time.

What This Book *Can't* Do:

- It can't write your book for you.
- It can't promise instant confidence or overnight success.
- It can't heal your trauma — but it can help you explore it safely, through words and awareness.
- It can't remove fear — but it can help you move with it.
- It can't make your story "perfect." (Because perfect isn't the point — truth is.)

If you use this book as a living practice — journaling through it, highlighting what resonates, reflecting honestly — you'll leave with more than a manuscript.

You'll leave with a deeper connection to yourself, your voice, and your purpose. This isn't just a writing guide. It's a **remembering**. And if you let it, it will lead you back to the writer you've always been.

WORKSHEET 0 — "MY COMMITMENT TO THE PAGE"
(TO BE COMPLETED BEFORE YOU BEGIN PART TWO)

This is your invitation to pause and set an intention before you begin.

Before you dive into structure, outlines, and publishing plans — take a moment to honor *why* you're here.

This isn't just a writing journey. It's a healing journey.

The words you are about to write will not only shape your story — they may also shape who you become.

Let this page be your gentle contract with yourself.

A promise to return — not to perfection, but to presence.

Not to performance, but to truth.

Take a deep breath. Place your hand over your heart.

And begin here.

✦ Why am I here?

(What called me to pick up this book? What season of life am I in right now?)

_____

_____

_____

✦ What do I hope writing will help me heal or understand?

(What parts of my story or emotions feel ready to be witnessed on the page?)

_____

_____

_____

✦ What promise do I want to keep to myself as I move through this book?

(What kind of energy do I want to bring to my writing practice?)

_____

_____

_____

✦ My Commitment

When I doubt, I will return.

When I resist, I will breathe.

When I fear, I will remember that courage is built one word at a time.

Affirmation:

"I commit to showing up for my story, one sentence at a time."

Signature: _____

Date: _____

PART TWO
THE COURAGE TO BEGIN
TURNING YOUR HEALING INTO WORDS THAT HELP OTHERS

CHAPTER 1
WRITING YOUR STORY AS A HEALING ACT

THE EMOTIONAL AND BIOLOGICAL BENEFITS OF STORYTELLING

Every story we carry has energy. Some of it moves freely — joy, gratitude, connection. But some gets stuck — grief, shame, fear, resentment — frozen in the body, looping through the nervous system long after the moment has passed.

When you sit down to write your story, you begin the brave and radical work of **moving that energy.** You turn unspoken experience into language, and in doing so, you give your pain somewhere to go.

Writing becomes both medicine and mirror: it helps you witness what was once unbearable — and, little by little, it loosens its hold.

For me, writing began in the middle of survival.

Not from a peaceful place of reflection, but from the mess —
the burnout, the sleepless nights, the feeling that my body and
mind were falling apart. The feeling that I was failing at life.

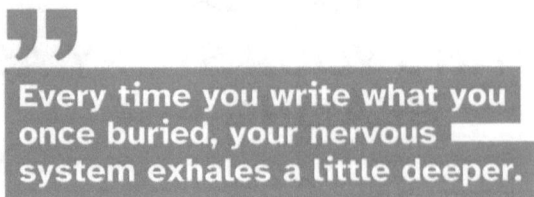

> **Every time you write what you
> once buried, your nervous
> system exhales a little deeper.**
>
> - Caroline Bakker

When I finally started putting my story on paper, I wasn't trying
to be profound. I was trying to just survive.

And that's what makes writing such a powerful act of healing
— it's not about becoming a writer (the truth is, I never set out
to be an author), it's about **reclaiming your voice** after years
of silencing yourself.

THE HEALING POWER OF STORYTELLING

Storytelling is ancient. Long before therapy existed, humans
healed by speaking around the fire. We shared stories of pain
and triumph, not just to remember, but to release.

**When we tell our stories — whether out loud or on the
page — we integrate what was fragmented.**

Modern neuroscience confirms what ancient wisdom has
always known: writing changes the brain.

Studies on **expressive writing**, pioneered by psychologist James W. Pennebaker, show that people who write about emotional experiences for just 15–20 minutes a day over several days experience stronger immune function, lower blood pressure, improved mood, and greater emotional clarity (Pennebaker, 1997; Pennebaker & Smyth, 2016).

Why? Because writing helps the brain **organize chaos into coherence.** When trauma or stress happens, our experiences are stored in disjointed fragments — sensations, images, emotions — without language.

By writing, we activate the prefrontal cortex (the part of the brain responsible for reasoning and meaning-making) while soothing the amygdala (the part that triggers fear and stress). This process helps regulate the body's stress response and improves emotional regulation (Lieberman et al., 2007).

In simple terms:

> *Writing tells your body,* "You're safe now. We can process this." *The moment you name what you feel, your nervous system exhales.*

HOW WRITING HELPS YOU PROCESS, INTEGRATE, AND TRANSFORM PAIN

There's a reason writing feels like medicine. When you put words to what once lived wordlessly inside you — the grief, the confusion, the memories that never had a place to land — something powerful begins to happen.

You're not just expressing emotion; you're reorganizing your inner world. You're giving language to energy that's been trapped in your body, sometimes for years.

This isn't only emotional healing — it's biological integration.

1. Processing:

Writing slows your thoughts down enough for you to witness them. Instead of cycling through the same worries or self-blame, you begin to see patterns and root causes. What once felt like chaos starts to take shape.

2. Integration:

Each time you tell your story, you link emotion with language, memory with meaning. It becomes less of a wound and more of a wisdom. The past stops hijacking the present.

3. Transformation:

Eventually, the page becomes a portal. The pain that once controlled you transforms into compassion — for yourself and others. What once silenced you now becomes your message.

That's the quiet miracle of writing: it turns survival into significance.

THE SCIENCE OF EXPRESSIVE WRITING — AND WHY IT WORKS

Pennebaker's decades of research on **expressive writing** found that translating emotional experiences into words improves both mental and physical health (Pennebaker, 1997; Pennebaker & Chung, 2011).

When we suppress emotion, the body carries the burden. But when we write, we activate both hemispheres of the brain — the analytical left and the emotional right — creating **integration across neural networks** (King, 2002).

Other studies by Dr. Matthew D. Lieberman at UCLA demonstrate that *affect labeling* — the simple act of naming emotions — literally reduces activity in the amygdala (the brain's fear center) and increases activity in the right ventrolateral prefrontal cortex, the region responsible for self-regulation (Lieberman et al., 2007). In other words, **writing regulates you.**

It bridges the mind-body gap by converting what's *felt* into what's *understood.* Even the act of handwriting has been shown to improve focus, strengthen memory, and support emotional regulation (Mangen & Velmans, 2020).

> Writing is where science meets the soul — it turns emotion into energy, chaos into coherence, and pain into meaning.

- Caroline Bakker

It's why journaling feels grounding — it anchors the intangible into something tangible. Writing, then, is not just self-expression. It's **self-regulation.** It's how we make sense of what the body remembers and the mind can't yet articulate.

WRITING AS NERVOUS SYSTEM REPAIR

For those of us living with ADHD, PMDD, trauma, or long-term stress, writing can become a form of **nervous system repair.**

It gives the body a rhythm — inhale, exhale, word, pause. It trains the brain to slow down, to observe, to reframe.

And it reminds us that our voice — the one that's been buried under conditioning, guilt, or exhaustion — still belongs to us.

When I started writing my first book, I didn't realize I was regulating my nervous system. But that's exactly what was happening.

Each sentence was a small act of coherence. Each paragraph, a reclamation of energy that had been stuck in survival mode.

Writing is not always easy. Sometimes it feels like reopening wounds. But what you're really doing is cleaning them — letting light in so they can heal properly.

Writing regulated me long before I understood the science — it taught my body that safety could be rebuilt, one sentence at a time.and pain into meaning.

- Caroline Bakker

A RADICAL ACT

We live in a world that tells us to move on, stay busy, numb the pain. So sitting down to write your truth — slowly, honestly, without a filter — is an act of rebellion.

It's saying:

> *"I refuse to rush my healing."*
> *"I refuse to pretend I'm fine."*
> *"I will give voice to what I was told to silence."*

Writing is radical because it demands presence. It invites honesty. And it transforms pain into purpose — not by erasing the past, but by redeeming it.

So when you pick up your pen or open your laptop, remember: **You're not just writing a book.**

You're reprogramming your body, reframing your story, and reminding yourself that your voice is medicine. That's not just creative work. That's healing work.

Reflection Prompt

What part of your story still feels heavy, confusing, or unfinished?

Write freely for ten minutes about it — no editing, no censoring, no structure.

Notice how your body feels before and after.

WORKSHEET 1 — STORY MEDICINE MAP

TO BE COMPLETED AFTER READING CHAPTER 1: WHY WRITING YOUR STORY IS A RADICAL ACT OF HEALING

Every story carries medicine — for you, and for someone else.

This page helps you uncover the experiences that shaped you most deeply, and begin to sense which one is asking to be written now.

There's no need to overthink it. Simply listen inwardly.

Notice what moments stir emotion, bring tears, or feel charged when you recall them. Those are often the places where your healing — and your writing — begins.

✦ Step 1 — Identify Three Defining Life Experiences

Think of three moments, seasons, or turning points that changed how you see yourself or the world.

They could be joyful, painful, ordinary, or extraordinary — what matters is that they *shifted something* inside you.

Life Experience	What Did I Learn?	How Did It Change Me?
1.		
2.		
3.		

✦ Step 2 — Circle One That Feels Ready to Be Told Now

Look at your three experiences.

Which one feels *alive* in your body when you read it? Which one carries a sense of readiness — not to re-live it, but to give it meaning?

Circle it, or underline it here:

The story that feels ready to be told now:

_____

(If none feel ready yet, that's okay. Trust the timing. This awareness is part of the process.)

✦ Step 3 — Reflection: The Ripple of Your Story

Every healing story carries a ripple. It travels far beyond you.

"If my story could heal one person, who would that be?"

Write their name, or describe the kind of person they are.

Is it someone like you, before your breakthrough?

Someone silently struggling with the same pattern, emotion, or diagnosis?

_____

_____

_____

_____

✦ Closing Intention

"The story I choose to write will be both my medicine and my offering."

Take a moment to sit with what surfaced.

You've just begun turning memory into meaning — and meaning into medicine.

CHAPTER 2
TURNING PAIN INTO POWER

HOW YOUR MOST DIFFICULT EXPERIENCES HOLD THE SEEDS OF PURPOSE

There's a reason certain memories linger. The ones that ache, replay, or surface in quiet moments are rarely random. They're invitations — signals from your soul pointing toward something unresolved, something that still holds energy, meaning, or medicine.

Your pain is not a mistake. It's data. It's information about where you lost connection to yourself, and it's the raw material through which purpose is born.

When we experience pain, especially the kind that breaks us open — loss, burnout, illness, heartbreak, identity crisis — we stand at a crossroads: **we can suppress it, spiritualise it away, or learn to transform it**.

Transformation begins when you stop asking, *"Why did this happen to me?"* and start asking, *"What is this trying to show me?"* That shift — **from victim to witness,** from pain to purpose — is what turns suffering into story.

When you begin to look at your life this way — not as a collection of random hardships, but as a curriculum of the soul — something shifts.

You realise that every experience that cracked you open was also shaping you. That your pain wasn't just meant to be survived, but translated.

And that translation begins with writing.

Writing is how we metabolise emotion into understanding. How we turn the invisible — the ache, the shame, the confusion — into something we can see, hold, and work with. It's where healing stops being an abstract concept and becomes embodied through language.

Because when you give your story form, you also give it meaning. And meaning is what turns wounds into wisdom.

THE ALCHEMY OF WRITING: TURNING EMOTION INTO MEANING

Alchemy is the art of transformation — turning base metals into gold. Writing does the same with emotion.

When you write honestly about your experiences, you take what was heavy and shapeless and begin to give it form. That act alone is healing. **You don't need to fix the past or make it pretty; you simply need to let it breathe on the page.**

Psychologist Viktor Frankl wrote that meaning, not happiness, is what allows humans to endure suffering. **"Those who have a *why* to live can bear almost any *how*."**

Writing is one way to uncover that *why*. When you tell your story, you begin to make sense of it — and when you make sense of it, you can finally release it. That's the alchemy of writing. You take pain, give it words, and it transforms into wisdom.

Writing is emotional alchemy. It's how we take what once broke us and turn it into something that breathes life — for ourselves, and for others.

- Caroline Bakker

Research in narrative psychology supports this process. Studies show that **"meaning-making"** through writing enhances post-traumatic growth, resilience, and emotional regulation (Park, 2010; Adler, 2012).

In other words, when you reframe your experience as a story of learning or service, your brain rewires the emotional memory — turning what was once trauma into a narrative of strength.

Each time you write about something difficult, you're teaching your nervous system: *This no longer controls me. I am the one telling the story now.*

MY STORY: FROM BURNOUT AND ADHD TO HEALING THROUGH WORDS

I didn't set out to be an author. I set out to get through the day. It was 2023. We had just moved from our dream property in the Macedon Ranges in Victoria, Australia — eight acres of eucalyptus trees, horses, and fresh air — to a high-rise apartment in Dubai.

My husband had recently survived emergency quintuple bypass surgery. My body was collapsing from eighteen months of sleep deprivation and postpartum depletion. I was burnt out, emotionally numb, and operating on **autopilot**.

I remember sitting on the bedroom floor, breastfeeding my daughter for the fourth time that night. The world outside glittered with city lights, but inside I felt invisible — a shell of the woman I used to be. That was when I self-diagnosed with ADHD.

Suddenly, so much made sense: the overwhelm, the emotional intensity, the chaos that lived in my mind (that I thought was normal). But naming it didn't fix it. I was still drowning.

So I did the only thing that had ever felt like oxygen. I wrote. Not for an audience. Not for a brand. Not for a best seller. Just to survive the night.

At first, it was messy — fragments, confessions, raw thoughts typed between toddler naps and midnight feeds. But then something began to shift.

The more I wrote, the less chaotic I felt. The noise in my head softened. The shame loosened. And my body, for the first time in years, began to exhale. Writing didn't erase my pain

— it *translated* it. **It turned emotional chaos into coherence.**

Neuroscience calls this process **"cognitive reappraisal"** — reframing experiences to regulate emotion and restore balance in the brain (Gross, 2015). But I call it *grace on the page*.

Each sentence became a small act of healing, each chapter a mirror showing me where I'd abandoned myself. And over time, those scattered pieces became something larger — a book. That book became *The Healing Journey*.

And in writing it, I discovered something I never expected: the act of turning pain into purpose isn't just about helping others — it's about reclaiming yourself.

THE RIPPLE EFFECT

When I finally shared parts of my story online, women began reaching out. One wrote:

> "Thank you for naming what I couldn't. I thought I was broken. Now I see I'm just human."

That's when I realised — our stories are never just ours. Every time we speak truth, we create resonance. We offer a mirror. And that mirror matters more than we know.

Empathy research shows that when people read personal narratives, the brain's **mirror neuron system** activates — the same circuits that light up when we experience emotion ourselves (Immordino-Yang et al., 2009).

In other words, when someone reads your story, their body *feels it.* Your healing literally communicates to their nervous system what's possible. That's the power of turning pain into words: **it doesn't just set you free — it frees others too.**

When I understood that — that my healing could ripple outward and touch others in ways I'd never see — everything about writing shifted.

It stopped being about achievement and started being about alignment. About service. About truth.

I realized that success isn't measured by numbers, followers, or reviews — it's measured by resonance. By the quiet, invisible transformations that happen in someone's heart because you had the courage to name what they couldn't.

And that realisation changed how I define success as an author.

REDEFINING SUCCESS

I used to think success as an author meant bestseller lists or thousands of sales. Now I know that success sometimes looks like one message from a stranger saying,

"I thought I was alone until I read your words."

It looks like the exhale you take after pressing *publish* — that moment your nervous system softens because you finally told the truth.

Writing isn't about being fearless. It's about being honest. And honesty, when shared, is power. Your story doesn't need to be dramatic to matter. It needs to be *true*.

So write it — not because you're ready, but because your body and soul are tired of holding it in.

Reflection Prompt

What experience in your life has shaped you the most — the one you rarely talk about, yet know changed everything?

Write about it as if you were speaking to someone who needs to hear they're not alone.

WORKSHEET 2 — PAIN TO PURPOSE ALCHEMY TABLE

TO BE COMPLETED AFTER READING CHAPTER 2: TURN YOUR PAIN INTO POWER

Alchemy isn't about erasing what happened. It's about transforming what once felt heavy into something useful, beautiful, and true.

Your story's power isn't found in perfection — it's found in perspective. When you look back through the eyes of growth, you begin to see how your pain shaped your purpose, your empathy, and your voice.

This table is your space to begin that transformation — from wound to wisdom, from experience to offering.

✦ Step 1 — Reflect on the Moments That Hurt, Changed, or Awakened You

Think of the experiences you identified in your *Story Medicine Map.*

Now, choose one or more to explore here.

Write honestly. Don't worry about eloquence. Let your truth speak first — the shaping will come later.

What Happened	What It Taught Me	How This Could Help Others
1.		
2.		
3.		

✦ Step 2 — Review Your Table

Read what you've written slowly. Notice any threads or recurring lessons.

Ask yourself:

- What patterns or themes do I see emerging?
- Where did strength, compassion, or clarity grow out of pain?
- How might sharing this experience give someone else hope or direction?

Circle or underline the insight that feels like the *heart* of your message.

✦ Step 3 — Anchor the Transformation

Transformation isn't about forgetting. It's about integration.

When we name the meaning inside our experiences, we reclaim the power we once gave away to pain.

Take a breath. Place your hand over your heart, and read this aloud:

Mantra:

"What once hurt now serves.

My story no longer defines me — it refines me."

✦ Optional Reflection

If you feel called, journal a few sentences below about how your story might ripple outward to help others.

✦ Closing Intention

"Today I choose to turn my pain into purpose — not by pretending it never hurt, but by choosing to make it matter."

CHAPTER 3
YOUR STORY AS SERVICE: HELPING OTHERS

Turning pain into purpose is a sacred act — but it's not a race.

Just because an experience shaped you doesn't mean it's ready to be shared. Healing has its own timeline. Some stories still need to rest in the dark before they can serve in the light.

That's where discernment comes in. Knowing *when* to tell your story is just as important as knowing *how*.

WRITING FROM THE SCAR, NOT THE WOUND

Not every story we live is ready to be told — at least, not yet. There's a difference between writing to heal and writing to help.

When I first started writing *The Healing Journey,* I wasn't trying to be an author. I was trying to survive.

I had just moved from Melbourne to Dubai with an 18-month-old who barely slept. I was navigating ADHD, PMDD (severe PMS), and the exhaustion of years of adrenal fatigue.

I began journaling in quiet pockets of the day — often on the floor, with my daughter napping beside me — just to make sense of the chaos inside.

Those early pages weren't meant for anyone else. They were my lifeline.

It took time — months of stillness, mindfulness, reading, and healing — before I could read those words without feeling the ache.

When I returned to them later, something had shifted: I no longer needed to write *about* the pain; I was writing *through* it, toward meaning. I realised that perhaps other women in this world would benefit from some of the revelations I had found.

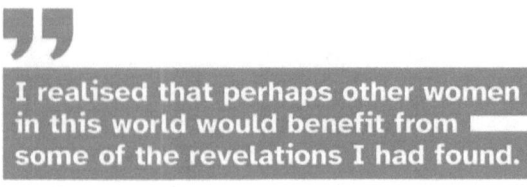

I realised that perhaps other women in this world would benefit from some of the revelations I had found.

- Caroline Bakker

That's when I knew I was ready to share. As psychologist **Dan McAdams** calls it, this is *narrative identity* — the ability to integrate painful events into a coherent story that gives life meaning (McAdams & McLean, 2013).

In neuroscience, this shift from chaos to coherence literally changes the structure of memory: emotional intensity fades while insight strengthens (Holland & Kensinger, 2010).

So before you share your story, ask yourself:

- Am I ready to hold space for others' reactions to this story?
- Can I talk about it without re-entering the pain?
- Do I understand the lesson this experience taught me?

If the answer is no, keep writing — but write privately. The page can hold your tears until they become truth. When the wound becomes a scar, it still tells the story, but it no longer bleeds when touched. **That's when you're ready to share**.

BALANCING VULNERABILITY AND WISDOM

When the wound becomes a scar, your story begins to change shape. It's no longer about survival — it's about service. But sharing from a healed place asks for something deeper than courage.

It asks for *wisdom* — the discernment to know how much of your truth to reveal, and how to hold it with care. That's where the art of balancing vulnerability begins.

Vulnerability is the heart of authentic writing. It's what lets readers feel you. It's what transforms information into intimacy — the space where a reader says, *"me too."*

But vulnerability, without grounding, can slip into self-exposure. Instead of serving the reader, it can leave *you* feeling unsafe or emotionally depleted.

When I wrote about PMDD rage in *The Healing Journey*, it took me several attempts to find the right tone. The first draft was raw — too raw. I could feel my nervous system tighten as I reread it. It wasn't ready. I was still too close to the experience, still bleeding through the words. So I set it aside.

Weeks later, after doing deeper healing work, I returned to that chapter. This time, I wrote from a calmer place — no longer as the woman inside the storm, but as the one who had found her way out.

The energy of the piece changed completely. It no longer felt like a cry for help; it felt like a hand reaching out. That rewrite became one of the most powerful sections of the book.

A woman messaged me months after it was published:

> *"Thank you. I thought I was a monster. Now I*
> *see I'm just a woman in pain."*

That message stopped me in my tracks. It reminded me that vulnerability, when shared from a grounded place, doesn't just connect — it heals.

That moment reminded me that writing isn't just about what we reveal — it's about what we choose to protect.

Our stories are living things. They deserve boundaries, patience, and timing. Before we share them with the world, we need to know which parts are ready to be seen and which still need our private care.

KNOWING WHEN TO SHARE (AND WHEN TO WAIT)

There's a fine line between vulnerability and exposure. The first connects you to others; the second leaves you feeling drained or unsafe. Sometimes you need to write from within the wound — but you don't need to publish from there.

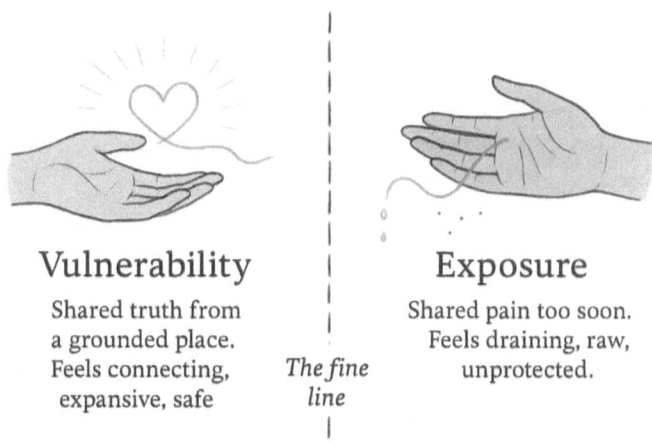

Vulnerability

Shared truth from
a grounded place.
Feels connecting,
expansive, safe

*The fine
line*

Exposure

Shared pain too soon.
Feels draining, raw,
unprotected.

When I began sharing about ADHD and PMDD publicly, I didn't post everything I wrote. Some pieces were too raw. They belonged in my journal or in conversations with one trusted friend.

Those early drafts became part of what I now call the middle layer — a safe testing ground where truth can breathe without the pressure of public eyes.

Later, after processing those emotions and integrating the lessons, I revisited those drafts and shaped them for my readers.

That's how they eventually became part of *The Healing Journey* — not as wounds, but as wisdom.

That's what Dr. Brené Brown talks about when she says that

> *"vulnerability without boundaries isn't*
> *vulnerability — it's oversharing."*

True vulnerability involves courage and discernment, grounded in emotional safety (Brown, 2012).

As writers, our deepest stories deserve time to mature — to transform from pain into perspective. When we share too soon, we invite sympathy. When we wait until we've healed, we offer strength.

"Time doesn't erase the truth — it refines it."

PRACTICAL WAYS TO STAY GROUNDED IN VULNERABILITY

If you're not sure whether a piece of writing is ready to be shared, pause and ask yourself:

- **Can I read this without my body tightening or my heart racing?**
  - If not, it's still for you — not for your audience yet.
- **Am I seeking validation or offering value?**
  - One comes from unhealed pain; the other from integrated wisdom.
- **Does sharing this feel empowering or exposing?**
  - The difference tells you which layer your story belongs in right now.

It can also help to:

- Write first, publish later — always give emotional space between creation and release.
- Check in with your body after you write; if you feel heavy or shaky, pause before sharing.
- Keep a trusted "witness" — a coach, friend, or therapist who can help you discern readiness.

Remember, your story doesn't lose power by waiting. It deepens. Time gives you clarity, perspective, and the ability to transform pain into purpose.

THE THREE LAYERS OF SHARING

Once you learn to listen to your body's cues and honor your own pace, you can begin to discern the layers of your story — what's for you, what's for a few, and what's ready for the world.

Here's a simple framework to help you hold that balance with clarity and care:

1. The Inner Layer — for you.

Private journals, notes, or unsent letters. This is your personal processing space — where emotion turns into understanding.

2. The Middle Layer — for those you trust.

Conversations with a therapist, writing coach, or close friend. This is where you begin to voice your truth safely and see how it lands.

3. The Outer Layer — for the world.

Your refined story, written from compassion and perspective. This is where your words become service — no longer about release, but connection.

When you share from the outer layer, your purpose shifts from *relief* to *resonance*. You write not to be seen, but to help others see themselves.

That is the art of vulnerable storytelling — truth told with tenderness, power, and peace. It's how pain becomes purpose, and experience becomes medicine. Because the stories we integrate are the ones that can truly heal.

WRITING FOR CONNECTION, NOT CATHARSIS

Catharsis — the release of pent-up emotion — has its place in healing, but it's only the first stage.

If you stop there, the writing stays self-focused. It becomes emotional dumping rather than meaningful storytelling.

Connection, on the other hand, requires perspective.

It transforms "this happened to me" into "this might help you."

The philosopher and psychologist **Carl Rogers** wrote that genuine empathy — the ability to sense another person's world as if it were your own — is the foundation of all healing communication (Rogers, 1961).

When you write from empathy, you stop performing your pain and start offering presence.

Here's how to make that shift:

- **Write in conversation with your reader.** Picture the one person who most needs to hear your story and speak directly to them.

- **Focus on universal emotions.** Instead of describing every event, highlight the feelings — fear, guilt, relief, hope — that anyone can relate to.

- **End with an offering.** What insight, question, or invitation can you leave them with? Healing stories don't just share; they *guide.*

Studies in narrative therapy show that when people craft stories of resilience and meaning, both the writer and the listener experience greater hope and empowerment (White & Epston, 1990; Angus & McLeod, 2004).

Your reader's nervous system responds to your story the way the body responds to music — syncing to the rhythm of your truth.

THE ENERGY OF SERVICE

When you write with the intention to serve, you activate a different part of yourself — the part that's no longer trapped in self-analysis but anchored in compassion.

Your words become a bridge. They carry your lessons across the divide between pain and purpose, helping others find their own way home.

Writing from service is the final step of integration: it completes the healing cycle. You receive the experience, you process it, you find its meaning, and then you release it into the world as wisdom.

This is what makes a healing author different from a diarist. You're not writing just to be heard — you're writing to help others hear themselves.

Reflection Prompt

Before you share your story, pause and ask:

Am I writing to heal, or writing to help?

If it still feels raw, let it rest.

When your words come from the scar, not the wound, they stop bleeding and start blessing.

WORKSHEET 3 — WOUND OR WISDOM CHECK-IN

TO BE COMPLETED AFTER READING CHAPTER 3: YOUR STORY AS SERVICE

Before you share your story with the world, it's essential to know *where* you're writing from.

Are you writing from a place that still aches — or from a place that has integrated the lesson?

Writing from a wound can reopen pain. Writing from wisdom helps others heal.

This worksheet isn't about judgment — it's about awareness.

It's your chance to check in with your nervous system and emotional readiness before stepping into visibility.

✦ Step 1 — Self-Reflection: Where Am I Writing From?

Read each statement below and mark the one that feels most true right now.

Statement	My Truth (✓)
I feel emotionally charged when I write about this experience.	
I often cry, shut down, or feel flooded when I revisit the memory.	
I can describe what happened, but it still feels raw or incomplete.	
I can talk about it calmly and reflectively, with some distance.	
I can identify what this experience taught me.	
I feel ready to use my story to help others, not just to process my pain.	

If your checkmarks fall mostly in the first three lines, it may be wise to spend more time healing privately before publishing publicly.

If they lean toward the bottom three, you're likely writing from a place of wisdom and integration.

Either way — you're exactly where you need to be.

✦ Step 2 — Grounding Before and After Writing

Writing about personal transformation activates the body. Grounding keeps your nervous system safe and steady.

Before you write:

1. Sit comfortably.
2. Take three slow breaths.
3. Feel your feet on the floor and imagine roots grounding you into the earth.
4. Whisper to yourself:
   - "I am safe in my body. My story is safe with me."

After you write:

1. Place a hand on your heart.
2. Inhale deeply and exhale slowly through the mouth.
3. Shake out your hands or stretch your body.
4. Repeat:
   - "I honor what surfaced and release what no longer needs to stay."

✦ Step 3 — Reflection Prompt

Write honestly, with no need for eloquence:

"What does readiness feel like in my body?"

_____

_____

_____

_____

"What boundaries or supports do I need in order to write safely?"

_____

_____

_____

_____

_____

✦ Step 4 — Intention Setting

Now, complete this gentle affirmation:

*"I give myself permission to share only what
feels grounded, integrated, and true.*

My story serves best when I honor my own healing first."

Signature: _____

Date: _____

CHAPTER 4
WHAT KIND OF BOOK ARE YOU WRITING?

Once you understand how to write from a place of service, the next step is to clarify what kind of book you're actually creating. Every healing story takes shape differently, and knowing the form helps you bring your message to life with intention, clarity, and confidence.

Before you begin, it helps to understand what you're truly writing—not to box yourself in with labels, but to create freedom through clarity.

You might already know this book is rooted in your personal story. But maybe you've wondered:

Is it a memoir?
Is it self-help?
Is it just journaling?
Or something else entirely?

Let me make this simple: You're not just writing about your life. You're writing about your *healing*. The book you're about to create is what I call **a healing book** — a blend of lived experience, insight, and transformation. It's part memoir, part guidebook, and part medicine for the reader's soul.

A healing book isn't about sharing every detail of your life — it's about sharing the *meaning* behind your experiences. It's the story *through* you, not just *about* you. You're not writing to be remembered. **You're writing to help someone else remember *themselves*.**

THE DIFFERENCE BETWEEN MEMOIR, SELF-HELP, AND A HEALING BOOK

As a child, I didn't really like reading. Looking back, it makes perfect sense — I had undiagnosed ADHD, and focusing for long stretches felt impossible unless the topic completely fascinated me.

Textbooks? Forget it. But give me a book about the mind, human potential, or spirituality, and I'd devour it.

When I first started thinking about writing my own book, I had no idea what category it would fall under. Fiction, nonfiction, memoir, self-help — those labels felt too rigid and academic. I didn't fit neatly into any of them.

I wasn't trying to write literature. I was trying to write *truth.* At that time, I was still deep in my own healing — burned out, newly diagnosed with ADHD, and navigating PMDD and motherhood.

What poured out of me wasn't "a manuscript." It was voice notes, journal entries, half-finished essays — pieces of emotion and awareness stitched together in real time.

It wasn't until later that I realized what I was writing was something different — not a memoir, and not a manual.

It was *a healing book.*

Every author begins with a story.

But what makes your book *healing* is not what happened to you — it's *how* you tell it, and *why.*

To help you see the difference clearly, here's a simple comparison:

What a Healing Book Is (and Isn't)

To help you see the difference clearly, here's a simple comparison:

Type of Book	What It Focuses On	Who It's For	How It Helps You (the Author)	How It Helps the Reader
Memoir	Your personal life story, told chronologically or thematically.	Readers curious about your experiences.	Helps you reflect and make sense of your past.	Offers inspiration and relatability through story.
Self-Help Book	Teaching frameworks, tools, and actionable strategies.	Readers seeking specific outcomes (like productivity, mindset, or success).	Positions you as an expert or guide.	Gives readers step-by-step change methods.
Fiction	Imagined stories, characters, and worlds.	Readers seeking entertainment or escape.	Expands your creativity and storytelling skills.	Allows emotional connection and meaning through story.
Healing Book	Your *real* experiences, transformed into insight, guidance, and hope.	Readers who are healing from something similar.	Helps you integrate your healing, give meaning to your journey, and reclaim your voice.	Offers readers validation, wisdom, and emotional transformation.

A **healing book** sits beautifully between memoir and self-help —it carries your story *and* your wisdom. It's personal enough to feel intimate, but practical enough to help the reader take action in their own life.

THE PURPOSE

A healing book blends the intimacy of memoir with the practicality of self-help. It's part story, part teaching, and entirely human. You're not writing to entertain or instruct — you're writing to connect. Your story becomes the bridge between what you've lived and what your reader is still navigating.

> When I began shaping The Healing Journey, I didn't set out to write a guide. But the more I wrote about my experiences with burnout, ADHD and PMDD, the more I realised I wasn't just telling my story — I was offering what I had learned.

That book became a conversation between my former self and the women who might still be there — overwhelmed, overstimulated, and unsure of where to begin. And that's exactly what a healing book does: **it extends a hand from your past self to someone else's present moment.**

FINDING YOUR CORE MESSAGE

Every healing book begins with one central idea — the heartbeat that ties everything together.

Your job is to find it. Maybe you already have a vague idea of your core message, or maybe you're completely overwhelmed. Here are some questions to ask yourself.

Ask yourself:

- What truth am I here to share?
- What problem or pain am I helping the reader understand or move through?
- If my reader walked away remembering just one thing, what would it be?

Your core message is the thread that keeps your book cohesive. It's what transforms a series of life events into a meaningful journey.

For example:

- "Healing isn't about fixing yourself — it's about remembering who you are."
- "Your nervous system holds the map back to your wholeness."
- "Writing your story is how you transform pain into purpose."

Once you know your message, every story, reflection, and lesson should point back to it.

When I was writing my first draft, I realized my message wasn't just about ADHD or PMDD — it was about *self-acceptance.* About learning to see myself with compassion instead of criticism. Once that truth became clear, the whole book aligned. Every chapter flowed from that one insight.

That's the power of a core message: it's your compass.

Once you've found your message, the next question becomes:

How will you tell it?

Because just as important as *what* you write is *how* your words feel when they land.

This is where your tone comes in.

WHAT TONE ARE YOU WRITING IN?

Before you decide on structure or outline, it helps to know what *voice* you want your book to speak in. Tone is the emotional undercurrent that carries your message—it's what makes your writing feel authentic, trustworthy, and alive.

When I began my first book, I had no idea what my tone was (or even what the word tone meant really). I just wrote whatever poured out—unfiltered, emotional, and sometimes all over the place. There was no structure yet, no clear direction. But that was okay. I needed to write messy before I could write meaningfully.

Often, you won't find your true tone until halfway through your manuscript—when your writing starts to sound more like you than like anyone else. When I was working in this book, it changed shape so many times and I didn't find my tone until 4 weeks before publishing it (yes this happens!).

Think of tone as the *frequency* your book vibrates on. It's what the reader feels beneath your words.

Is it calm and reflective? Honest and raw? Encouraging and instructional?

Your tone sets the emotional contract between you and your reader.

THE THREE COMMON TONES OF HEALING BOOKS

Every healing story carries its own rhythm — some pages feel like a heartfelt conversation, others like a guided reflection or a teaching moment. Understanding these tones will help you shape how your story is received and how your reader feels held as they move through it.

1. **The Storyteller's Tone**: Personal, honest, poetic. It feels like sitting down with a friend over tea. You share lessons through lived experience, not instruction.

Best for memoir-style chapters or when you want to build deep emotional connection.

2. **The Guide's Tone**: Practical, empowering, clear. You speak directly to the reader as a mentor, giving steps, reflections, or tools to apply.

Best for sections with frameworks, exercises, or teaching moments.

3. **The Teacher-Healer Tone**: A fusion of both. It carries story, science, and soul in equal measure. You reveal your process, offer tools, and hold the reader with compassion.

This is the tone most healing authors grow into—it's what makes your writing both relatable and transformative.

HOW TO FIND YOUR TONE

Ask yourself:

- What do I want my reader to *feel* while reading my book?
- How would I speak if I were mentoring one person sitting across from me?
- What energy do I want to leave behind—calm, fire, hope, or faith?

Write a few paragraphs in different tones. Try one that sounds like a journal entry, one like a letter to a friend, and one like you're teaching a workshop. Read them aloud. The one that makes you feel most like *yourself*—that's your tone.

Don't overthink it. You'll refine it through writing. Your tone will evolve, just as you do, from raw emotion to embodied wisdom. And when that happens, your book won't just read beautifully —it will *feel true.*

THE READER'S MIRROR MOMENT

In every healing story, there's a moment when the reader sees themselves in your words.

It's the mirror — the reflection that whispers, *"Me too."*

That's the moment transformation begins.

The goal of your book isn't to impress the reader with your resilience — it's to include them in it.

The most powerful healing books create space for the reader's story alongside yours.

When I began hearing from readers of *The Healing Journey*, I noticed something: they weren't quoting my advice; they were reflecting on their *own* lives.

One woman wrote, "Your chapter on emotional regulation made me realize how disconnected I've been from my body."

That was my mirror moment — realizing that my story had become a portal for someone else's self-awareness.

Research in narrative psychology calls this **self-referential resonance** — when readers internalize another person's story as a catalyst for their own growth (McLean et al., 2007).

In simpler terms: your story becomes a permission slip for someone else to begin theirs.

To create this resonance:

- Share emotions, not just events.
- Include reflection questions or journaling prompts.
- Speak *to* the reader, not *at* them.

You're not the hero of your story — the reader is.

You're the guide who helps them find the courage to face their own.

THE HEALING BOOK STRUCTURE: STORY → LESSON → INVITATION

Most healing books follow a simple yet powerful rhythm:

1. Story — Share the experience: This is your lived moment: what happened, how it felt, what you went through. Be real, not polished.

2. Lesson — Reflect on what it taught you.: What insight emerged? What truth did you uncover? What shifted inside you?

3. Invitation — Turn the mirror toward the reader.: Ask a question, offer a tool, or extend a reflection they can take into their own life.

This structure creates emotional movement: it draws the reader in, grounds them in meaning, and leaves them with something transformative.

For example:

- **Story:** "When I was deep in burnout, I thought rest was weakness."
- **Lesson:** "Now I know that rest is the foundation of resilience."
- **Invitation:** "Where are you still equating rest with guilt? What would happen if you gave yourself permission to stop?"

This approach turns a personal anecdote into a shared healing experience.

From a psychological perspective, this mirrors the three stages of **post-traumatic growth** identified by Tedeschi and Calhoun (2004): understanding, meaning-making, and action.

When we write (or read) in this way, we move through the same stages —

- Understanding what happened,
- Finding meaning in it, and
- Taking action through new awareness.

That's why this structure feels so natural: it mirrors the very process of healing itself.

When You Write This Way, your book stops being *your story.* It becomes *our story.* And that's when it starts to heal.

Reflection Prompt

What is the core message behind your story?

Write one sentence that captures the truth you want your reader to carry when they close the final page.

Then ask yourself: How can I weave that message through every chapter — through story, lesson, and invitation?

WORKSHEET 4 — BOOK IDENTITY COMPASS

TO BE COMPLETED AFTER READING CHAPTER 4: WHAT KIND OF BOOK ARE YOU WRITING?

Every healing book begins with a heartbeat — but it also needs direction. This worksheet will help you define *what kind* of book you're creating, *who* it's for, and *what transformation* it offers.

Think of it as your inner compass: a way to find clarity before you get lost in chapters and outlines.

✦ Step 1 — Understanding the Three Paths

Use this table to sense which format feels most aligned with your story. There's no wrong answer — many healing authors blend these elements into something uniquely their own.

Type of Book	Core Focus	Voice + Tone	Reader's Expectation	Best Suited For You If...
Memoir	Personal story told through scenes and reflection	Intimate, emotional, narrative	Wants to be moved or inspired by your lived journey	You're called to tell your story as it unfolded, focusing on emotional truth rather than teaching
Self-Help / Guide	Practical tools, frameworks, and advice	Clear, structured, teacherly	Seeks actionable strategies or change	You enjoy teaching, breaking things down, or guiding readers through steps
Healing Book (Hybrid)	Story woven with insight and invitation	Conversational, vulnerable, wise	Wants both connection *and* transformation	You want to merge story and service — to help readers heal through your lived example

Now, circle or highlight the type that feels most like *home* for your book. Or write your hybrid version here:

My book is a blend of:

_____

_____

✦ Step 2 — Define Your Core Message

Every healing book can be summarized in one clear sentence — the truth you most want readers to remember.

"If my reader remembers just one thing after closing my book, it's that…"

_____

_____

_____

_____

_____

_____

(Keep this statement visible while writing. It becomes your North Star.)

✦ Step 3 — Your Reader's Mirror Moment

Imagine your ideal reader — the person who picks up your book in the middle of a difficult season.

Write a few lines describing them:

- What are they struggling with?
- What are they longing for?
- How do you want them to feel by the final page?

_____

_____

Now complete this sentence:

"My book meets my reader where they are in their pain — and walks them toward _____."

_____

_____

_____

✦ Step 4 — The Healing Book Structure

Every great healing book follows a natural rhythm:

Story → Lesson → Invitation

Chapter Element	Description	Example
Story	A scene, moment, or reflection from your life.	"The morning I realized burnout wasn't weakness — it was a message."
Lesson	The insight, science, or wisdom that reframed that moment.	"I learned that the body's exhaustion is the nervous system begging for safety."
Invitation	A reflection, question, or exercise for the reader.	"What message is your body trying to send you today?"

_____

_____

_____

Use this pattern to build flow in each chapter — it keeps your writing personal, purposeful, and transformative.

✦ Step 5 — Reflection Prompt

"What kind of transformation do I want my book to create — in me, and in my reader?"

_____

_____

_____

_____

_____

✦ Closing Intention

"My story is the bridge between my experience and my reader's healing.

I will write not to impress, but to impact."

Signature: _____

Date: _____

CHAPTER 5

HOW TO START (EVEN WHEN IT'S MESSY)

START MESSY. STAY CONSISTENT. LET IT EVOLVE.

Most people think they need confidence, clarity, or the perfect writing plan before they start their book. But the truth is—you **begin before you feel ready.**

Every author you admire once sat in front of a blank page wondering if their words would matter. None of them had it all figured out. They simply followed a pull — a whisper that said, *Start here. Start now.*

When I began *The Healing Journey*, I didn't have an outline or even a title. I had a deep urge to make sense of what I'd lived through and a quiet hope that it might help someone else. What mattered wasn't *how* I started — it was that I did.

Writing a healing book isn't about waiting for confidence. It's about building it — sentence by sentence.

You can't think your way into readiness; you have to *write* your way there.

Neuroscience shows that **action precedes motivation**, not the other way around. Each time you take a small step — even opening your document — your brain releases dopamine, rewarding the act of beginning. **That tiny spark of momentum becomes the fuel that carries you forward**.

OVERCOMING FEAR, PERFECTIONISM, AND PROCRASTINATION

Most aspiring authors live in the space between inspiration and fear.

You feel the whisper that says, *It's time*, and then resistance crashes in.

Who am I to write a book?
What if no one reads it?
What if I can't finish?
What if I embarrass myself?

That's not laziness. That's fear wearing a thousand disguises — fear of being seen, judged, or not being good enough.

Psychologists **Fuschia Sirois** and **Timothy Pychyl** found that procrastination isn't a time-management issue; it's an *emotion regulation* issue — an attempt to avoid uncomfortable feelings like anxiety or inadequacy (Sirois & Pychyl, 2013).

Perfectionism is no different. It's not ambition gone wild; it's a self-protective mechanism. Perfectionism activates the same stress circuits as social threat, keeping us hypervigilant (Stoeber & Otto, 2006).

During the early months of writing, my perfectionism disguised itself as "research." I spent hours comparing fonts and Canva mock-ups. It felt productive, but really, it was fear in a prettier outfit. Once I recognized that, I made myself a rule: **research after writing.**

Psychologist Carol Dweck calls this the *growth mindset* — the belief that abilities develop through effort rather than innate talent (Dweck, 2006). If your goal is to "feel ready," you'll wait forever. If your goal is to learn as you go, you've already begun.

Fear doesn't mean you're unqualified — it means you're doing something that matters. Let that tremor be your compass.

Once you've named your fears and loosened perfectionism's grip, you create space for movement.

Clarity doesn't come before action — it comes *through* it. The antidote to fear isn't confidence; it's momentum.

So let's turn that energy into something tangible. Here's how to begin — one grounded, gentle step at a time.

HOW TO START (STEP BY STEP)

There's no single right way to begin, but there *is* a way forward — one grounded in simplicity, embodiment, and consistency.

Start small. Start where you are.

Step 1 — Create Your Container

Before you worry about words, build your space.

- Open a folder or grab a new notebook titled **"My Book."**
- Inside, create three simple files: *Ideas*, *Stories*, and *Lessons*.

This becomes your creative container — a home for everything that wants to come through.

Step 2 — Set an Intention

Before you write, pause and ask:

> *"What do I want this book to give — to me, and to others?"*

Write your answer at the top of your document.

That intention becomes your compass when doubt creeps in.

Step 3 — Brain Dump Without Editing

Spend fifteen minutes free-writing whatever wants to emerge — memories, emotions, moments, fragments. Don't edit or judge. You're gathering raw material, not polishing diamonds.

Step 4 — Capture Real Moments

Go back through old journals, photos, or voice notes. Revisit the scenes that shaped you. Ask yourself: *What was I feeling? What did I learn?* That's where your emotional truth lives.

Step 5 — Pick One Story to Expand

Choose a single moment that feels alive and start there. Write it like you're telling it to a trusted friend. Honesty matters more than structure.

Step 6 — Schedule Micro-Sessions

Consistency beats intensity.

- Choose three short windows each week — even twenty minutes counts.
- Protect them like sacred appointments.

Your muse learns to trust you when you show up.

Step 7 — End with Gratitude

After every session, whisper:

"That was enough for today."

Gratitude rewires your brain to associate writing with calm, safety, and reward.

Once you've built a simple structure to begin, the next step is to make writing feel less like a checklist and more like a ceremony.

Because healing writing doesn't thrive on discipline alone — it needs rhythm, tenderness, and trust. That's where ritual comes in.

WRITING AS A RITUAL, NOT A TASK

Once you stop waiting for confidence, your next step is to create rhythm — not pressure. Rituals tell your nervous system, *You're safe to create.*

Here are the rituals that kept me grounded while writing:

- **Create a Sensory Anchor**: Light a candle or brew cacao before writing (I have ceremonial grade cacao every day). Let scent or taste signal safety and focus.
- **Start Small, Stay Consistent:** Some days I wrote for fifteen minutes before bed; other days for two hours. Both mattered.
- **Write First, Edit Later:** Your first draft is *discovery*, not *delivery.* Editing too early kills flow.
- **Honor Your Energy Cycles:** I wrote best in my follicular phase and rested during my luteal phase. Aligning creativity with your hormones changes everything.(more about that in the following section, writing with the body mind and cycle).
- **Protect the Sacred Space:** Turn off notifications, close tabs, and let loved ones know you're writing. Even twenty focused minutes moves the needle (use the pomodoro technique).

Rituals aren't about productivity. They're about embodiment —

the felt experience of being fully present in your creative energy.

Rituals create the space. Consistency keeps it alive. Once you've built a rhythm that feels nourishing instead of pressured, what matters most is not how inspired you feel — but that you return.

Because creativity doesn't respond to force; it responds to familiarity. **Each time you show up, your body learns: it's safe to write here.**

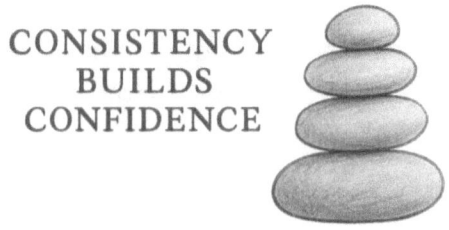

CONSISTENCY
BUILDS
CONFIDENCE

THE IMPORTANCE OF CONSISTENCY OVER CONFIDENCE

Confidence doesn't precede writing — it *comes* from writing. **Each act of showing up is an investment in self-trust.**

In behavioral psychology, this is called *habit stacking* (Clear, 2018). Link writing to an existing habit — morning tea, nap time, or after dinner. When writing becomes part of your rhythm, it stops being a question and becomes a practice.

Your goal isn't perfection. It's *returning*. Some days you'll write one sentence. Other days, five pages. Both count.

Because writing, like healing, is cumulative. The more you return, the safer it feels to express — and one day, you'll look back at your messy notes and realize: you were writing your book all along.

WHEN RESISTANCE SHOWS UP

It will. Even the most disciplined writers meet days when everything in them wants to run. When that happens, pause and ask:

"What am I afraid to feel right now?"

Often, the hardest part isn't writing the story — it's *feeling* it. On those days, I don't force myself. I move. Stretch. Breathe. Walk.

Writing is body work as much as brain work. Resistance isn't failure — it's initiation. Your nervous system is expanding to hold more truth, more visibility, more power.

When you meet it with curiosity instead of judgment, it transforms into flow.

WHEN IS YOUR BOOK FINISHED?

Most writers focus so much on *how to start* that they forget the question that quietly waits at the other end: *How do I know when it's done?*

If you're anything like me, you'll never feel like your book is completely finished. Each time I printed *The Healing Journey*, I found more to refine — a sentence to tighten, a new study to cite, a better way to express what I meant. I printed it four times before publication, tweaking, improving, and polishing because I wanted it to feel *complete*. But completion is a moving target.

Books, like people, evolve. What feels finished today may reveal new depth a year from now — and that's the point. Each version of your work reflects the level of wisdom and consciousness you hold in that season of your life. It doesn't need to be perfect; it needs to be honest.

The goal isn't to write the perfect book — it's to capture the truth of where you are, knowing you'll meet it again from a higher place.

- Caroline Bakker

Eventually, you realize that perfection isn't the goal — *impact is*. Your job is to give the book everything you can *for now* and then release it. Let it live. Let it meet the people who need it.

When I finally hit "Publish," I didn't feel done. I felt *released*. I had done my best with what I knew, and that was enough.

Here's what helped me decide:

1. **Print it.** Holding your book in your hands changes everything. You'll see what needs refining — and feel when it's ready.

2. **Rest, then revisit.** Step away for a week. Return with fresh eyes. If the message still moves you, it's ready.

3. **Ask, "Does this serve?"** If your words help the reader you wrote for, you've done your job.

4. **Remember, you can always evolve.** New insights, research, or stories can live in your next edition. Growth doesn't invalidate your earlier work — it honors it.

Perfectionism keeps you polishing forever. Courage lets you share it anyway. So write your truth, refine it with love, and then — let it go. **Because your book can't heal anyone while it's still sitting on your desktop.**

Pro tip: Being a perfectionist myself, and having limiting beliefs such as "it's never going to be good enough" didn't help me. Awareness did. Awareness of my limiting beliefs helped me transform them - and helped me release my book when it was 80% good. Because out there, is better than perfect. It also shows the reader you're human.

YOUR HEALING DOESN'T REQUIRE PERFECTION

Writing your story is not an act of control — it's an act of courage. Your words don't need to be polished. They need to be *true*. Every messy sentence brings coherence to your inner world. Every paragraph builds a bridge between your past and your purpose. The only mistake is not starting.

So start messy. Start scared. Start today.

WORKSHEET 5 — "DAILY WRITING RITUAL BLUEPRINT

TO BE COMPLETED AFTER READING CHAPTER 5: HOW TO START (EVEN WHEN IT'S MESSY)

You don't need perfect conditions to write. You need *safe* ones.

This worksheet will help you create a daily or weekly writing rhythm that works with your life — not against it.

Your ritual doesn't have to be long or complicated. It's about consistency, not perfection.

Think of it as building a small, sacred doorway that you can walk through every time you return to the page.

✦ Step 1 — Create Your Writing Container

Ritual Element	My Intention	Notes or Ideas
Time	What time of day feels most peaceful or realistic for me to write?	
Duration	How long will i write when I show up (even if short)?	
Place	Where in my home, nature, or daily routine will I write?	
Anchor Object	Candle, essential oil, playlist, cup of tea — what sensory cue will remind my body it's time to write?	
Closing Ritual	How will I signal to myself that my writing time is complete (stretch, breath, affirmation)?	

✦ Step 2 — Grounding Before You Begin

Before writing, take 60 seconds to anchor your body and breath.

This helps you regulate your nervous system so you can write from presence, not pressure.

1. Sit or stand tall. Feel your feet on the ground.
2. Take a slow inhale for 4 counts. Exhale for 6.
3. Whisper your mantra aloud:
   - "My story is medicine. I am safe to speak it."
4. Begin — even if you only write one line.

✦ Step 3 — The Write Anyway Practice

When your mind says, "I don't have time," or "It's not good enough," try the **10-Minute Write Anyway Timer.**

Set a timer for 10 minutes.

Write without stopping, editing, or censoring.

Even if it's a single word repeated.

Even if all you can manage is: *"I don't know what to say."*

Momentum builds through permission, not pressure.

✦ Step 4 — Track Your Writing Energy (Optional)

Use this mini log to observe patterns in your focus, mood, or environment.

Use this mini log to observe patterns in your focus, mood, or environment.				
Date	How long I wrote	My mood before	My mood after	Notes / Insights

Notice what supports your creativity best — time of day, music, location, or emotional state.

✦ Step 5 — Reflection Prompt

"When I think about writing as a sacred practice rather than a task, how does it change the way I show up?"

_____

_____

_____

_____

_____

✦ Closing Intention

"Perfection isn't my job. Presence is.

My words don't have to be beautiful — they just have to be honest."

Signature: _____

Date: _____

PART THREE
WRITING WITH THE BODY, MIND & CYCLE

A HOLISTIC FRAMEWORK FOR SUSTAINING CREATIVITY AND HEALTH AS A HEALING WRITER.

CHAPTER 6
WRITING THROUGH
THE BODY
HOW YOUR BODY BECOMES YOUR
CREATIVE INSTRUMENT

W hen I first began writing *The Healing Journey*, I thought creativity lived mostly in the mind — in discipline, focus, and word count goals.

But what I learned, sometimes the hard way, is that creativity lives in the **body**. Every sentence you write is filtered through your nervous system, your hormones, your breath, and your heartbeat.

Your body holds every memory you've ever lived, and every story you've yet to tell. If it's tense, depleted, or inflamed, your words will carry that frequency. If it's nourished, rested, and open, your writing will flow with ease.

Writing became a mirror for how well I was caring for myself — or how much I was still pushing from the old patterns of perfectionism and survival.

THE BODY REMEMBERS THE STORY

For years, I tried to out-think my body. I pushed through exhaustion, numbed discomfort with caffeine, and measured my worth by how much I could produce. When I was diagnosed with ADHD and later began to understand my PMDD patterns, everything started to make sense. My body wasn't failing me—it was communicating.

The mood swings, brain fog, and fatigue were not random obstacles to productivity; they were messages. They were my nervous system begging me to slow down, to process the emotion I had carried for years, to integrate the trauma I had intellectualized but never released.

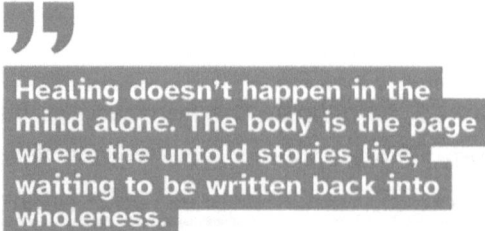

Healing doesn't happen in the mind alone. The body is the page where the untold stories live, waiting to be written back into wholeness.

- Caroline Bakker

As psychiatrist **Bessel van der Kolk** explains in *The Body Keeps the Score*, trauma is not stored as a memory to be reasoned with but as a lived experience encoded in the body. It shapes posture, breathing, digestion, and sleep until it is acknowledged and moved through the nervous system. Similarly, **Dr. Gabor Maté** reminds us in *When the Body Says No* that the chronic suppression of emotion can manifest as physical illness; what the mind resists feeling, the body is forced to express.

Trauma doesn't disappear simply because you understand it. It lodges in fascia, muscle tension, digestion, and sleep patterns until you learn to move it. Writing helped me begin that release, but it was through bodywork—movement, breath, and stillness —that the stories truly transformed.

Every time I sat down to write about something painful, my shoulders would tighten and my jaw would clench. My body remembered what my mind wanted to forget. The healing began when I stopped fighting that response and started listening to it.

Listening to my body was only the beginning.

Once I learned to honor its messages, I started to see that healing wasn't just emotional — it was biochemical. Every feeling, every word, every burst of creativity required energy at the cellular level. My nervous system could only integrate what my body had the vitality to sustain. **That realisation changed everything.**

ENERGY AS THE NEW CURRENCY

After years of running on adrenaline, my body finally said "enough." I was deep in adrenal fatigue — living on stress hormones, caffeine, and sheer willpower.

That collapse forced me to look at energy in an entirely new way — not as a matter of time management, but as *cellular vitality*.

My husband has worked in the health and wellness industry for more than twenty years, and I've been part of this world for over a decade myself. As mentioned earlier, in 2023, we moved our family from Melbourne to Dubai to set up a clinic focused on precision health, longevity, functional medicine, and genetic optimization. Our mission was simple: **to help people heal at the root level by understanding their biology**.

I did my first DNA test back in 2019, long before genetic health became popular. But as the technology evolved and testing became more advanced, I decided to repeat it through **Nordic Laboratories**, one of Europe's leading functional medicine testing providers. This time, the results gave me deeper insight into *why* my body functioned the way it did.

What Functional Medicine and Genetic Optimization Mean

Functional Medicine looks at the root causes of health issues rather than just treating symptoms. Instead of asking, "What pill matches this problem?" it asks, "Why is this happening in the first place?" It combines science and systems biology to understand how your organs, hormones, and lifestyle interact — so healing can happen from the ground up.

Genetic Optimization means using your DNA as a roadmap. Through a simple saliva or blood test, you can identify small variations (called SNPs, or single nucleotide polymorphisms) that influence how your body processes nutrients, hormones, and stress. Once you know these patterns, you can tailor your nutrition, supplements, and lifestyle choices to support your biology — rather than work against it.

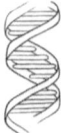

I discovered several genetic variants — including **MTHFR** and **COMT** — that explained why I was more sensitive to stress, slower to process certain nutrients, and prone to emotional burnout. In simple terms, these variants are like small spelling differences in your genetic code that can influence how efficiently your body converts nutrients into usable forms and clears neurotransmitters like dopamine and adrenaline. When these pathways are sluggish, even the healthiest diet or supplement plan might not be enough — your body simply can't use what you give it.

Once I began supporting these pathways with the right forms of nutrients — methylated B12 and folate to support methylation, magnesium glycinate to calm my nervous system, omega-3s for brain health, and vitamin D for hormone balance — everything began to shift. My focus returned. My moods steadied. And my creativity — that quiet pulse I thought I'd lost — came back stronger than ever.

Creative burnout doesn't begin on the page; it begins in the **mitochondria** — the tiny engines inside your cells that produce ATP, or adenosine triphosphate, your body's true energy currency. When those engines are deprived of rest, nutrients, or recovery, no amount of motivation can override biology.

Today, I treat energy as my most sacred resource. I no longer trade it for urgency or external validation. I protect it like the muse itself depends on it — because it does.

If you're curious to learn more about your own genetics or how DNA testing can help you understand your unique energy blueprint, you can reach out to me directly. I'd be happy to connect you with our Dubai-based clinic team and help you explore what's possible for your health.

MOVEMENT AS MEDICINE

Once I began rebuilding my energy from the inside out, I realized healing doesn't end with nutrition or supplements — it continues through movement.

Energy wants to move. When it stagnates, creativity stalls, emotion lingers, and the body begins to tighten again.

For me, the next phase of healing wasn't just biochemical; it was *kinetic*— healing through movement, breath, and the body in motion.

Before I became an author, I was a boxer and fitness coach. Movement taught me discipline, but more than that, it taught me presence. When you're in the boxing ring, there's no space for distraction — you have to feel every signal from your body.

That somatic awareness became the foundation of my writing practice.

When I returned to writing after burnout, I realised my words flowed best after I moved my body. A walk around the block, a few minutes of stretching, or even gentle shaking could release the static that built up from sitting too long.

Later, acupuncture became another form of movement for me — energy moving through meridians, tension dissolving where stories once hid. Sauna sessions helped me sweat out the emotional residue of intense writing days. The more I honored movement, the more alive my creativity felt.

Stillness has its place, but movement keeps the stories from stagnating. Creativity is circulation — physical, emotional, and energetic.

Movement taught me how to release energy; rest taught me how to restore it.

The more I honored my body's need for motion, the more I began to understand its equal need for recovery. Healing — like creativity — isn't just about how much energy you generate, but how wisely you regulate it.

That awareness led me to the next layer of my healing practice: aligning with my body clock.

REST AS RHYTHM: ALIGNING WITH YOUR BODY'S CLOCK

Movement taught me how to release energy; rest taught me how to restore it.

For years, I saw sleep as the thing that came *after* the work was done. But when I was recovering from burnout, I realized sleep *was* the work — the invisible foundation that everything else depended on.

When I began tracking my sleep with the **Oura Ring** in 2019, I started noticing patterns that mirrored my mental and emotional states. On nights I stayed up late writing under bright screens, my data would show elevated heart rate, delayed recovery, and fragmented rest. The next morning, my mind felt foggy, sentences clunky, and emotions raw. It wasn't just fatigue — it was a full nervous system dysregulation.

In my book *The Healing Journey: Navigating Adult ADHD & PMDD*, I wrote about how people with ADHD often struggle with sleep due to dopamine imbalances, irregular light exposure, and racing thoughts. Those same patterns affect creativity. When the brain's circadian rhythm — its natural 24-hour clock — falls out of sync, your focus, mood, and energy follow.

You might recognize the signs:

- Feeling wired late at night but sluggish in the morning.
- Crashing mid-afternoon and relying on caffeine to push through.
- Bursts of inspiration at 11 p.m., followed by insomnia.

That's not a lack of discipline — it's a biological rhythm that's lost its beat.

The good news is, your body's clock can be reset through simple, sensory cues. Here's what worked for me — and what I now teach my clients and readers to help them reconnect with their natural creative rhythm.

Morning: Light Before Screens

Before checking your phone, step outside for 10–15 minutes of sunlight.

Natural light activates the **suprachiasmatic nucleus** in your brain — your body's internal clock — signaling that it's time to wake up. This gentle light exposure triggers a healthy rise in **cortisol** (for alertness) and sets the timer for **melatonin** (for sleep) about 14–16 hours later.

Screens, by contrast, deliver dopamine spikes and stress hormones before your nervous system has even oriented to the day. Sunlight, not notifications, is what tells your body: *You're safe to begin.*

Daytime: Move Every 90 Minutes

Your brain operates in **ultradian rhythms** — natural 90–120 minute cycles of energy, focus, and rest. After about an hour and a half of deep work, your physiology starts to shift: oxygen levels drop, dopamine dips, and focus wanes. That's your cue to move.

A walk, stretch, or few deep breaths restores circulation and rebalances your stress hormones. Movement mid-day isn't a distraction from creativity — it's what keeps your ideas alive.

Evening: Dim the Day Away

As the sun sets, your body expects darkness. Bright artificial light — especially from blue screens — tricks your brain into thinking it's still daytime, suppressing **melatonin** and delaying your sleep window.

I now dim lights after sunset, switch to amber filters on devices, and replace scrolling with journaling. Magnesium tea helps calm the nervous system and ease the transition into rest. This single ritual restored both my sleep and my writing flow.

Why Rhythm Fuels Creativity

Your circadian rhythm isn't just about rest; it's the architecture of creative flow.

When your body's internal clock is stable, **cortisol**, **dopamine**, and **melatonin** rise and fall in harmony — supporting attention, emotional regulation, and imagination.

When it's unstable, the nervous system stays stuck in fight-or-flight, making focus, clarity, and inspiration harder to access.

When I finally honored my body's natural cycles, my creativity stopped feeling forced. Words began to arrive with ease. The muse, I realized, loves regulation.

Consistent sleep became the silent editor of my work — refining ideas, consolidating memories, and connecting insights that only rest can weave together.

Your body's natural rhythm follows the same creative curve throughout the day — rising with morning light, peaking with mid-day focus, and softening into evening rest.

The illustration below maps this 24-hour cycle of light, hormones, and energy — showing how each phase supports a different aspect of your creative and emotional wellbeing.

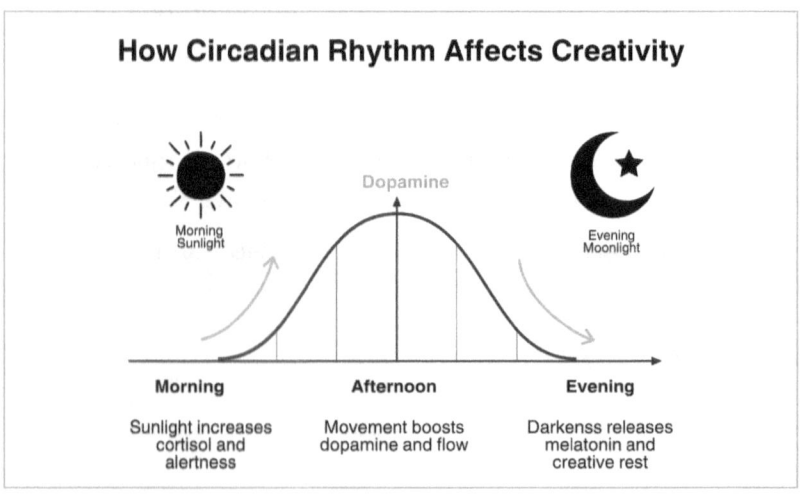

In the **morning**, exposure to sunlight tells your brain it's time to wake up. Light triggers a healthy rise in **cortisol**, the hormone that promotes alertness and motivation. This is when your energy, focus, and executive function are at their sharpest —

the ideal time for structured writing, planning, or problem-solving.

By **afternoon**, your body settles into a natural rhythm of movement and flow. Physical activity or even short walks boost **dopamine**, the neurotransmitter linked to curiosity, inspiration, and creative insight. This is your optimal window for brainstorming, expression, and drafting — the stage of creative play and movement.

As **evening** arrives, darkness signals your pineal gland to release **melatonin**, helping your body and mind wind down. This phase invites integration — journaling, reflection, or reading. During sleep, your brain consolidates memories, processes emotions, and forms new neural connections, turning today's experiences into tomorrow's wisdom.

When you live and create in sync with this rhythm, you stop fighting your biology and start flowing with it.

You give your body permission to rest, your mind space to integrate, and your creativity room to breathe. Because healing, like writing, isn't about intensity — it's about rhythm.

REFLECTION: LISTENING TO THE BODY'S WISDOM

Your body is the first draft of every story you'll ever write. It speaks through energy, movement, tension, sleep, and silence — long before words ever reach the page.

If you've ever felt blocked, burned out, or disconnected from your creative voice, it's not because you've lost it. It's because your body is asking for alignment. Every pause, every ache, every moment of fatigue carries a message: *slow down, breathe, come home.*

As you move forward in your writing journey, remember that healing isn't separate from creativity — it's what allows creativity to unfold.

Care for your body as you would care for your manuscript.

Rest when you need to. Move when energy builds. Listen when stillness calls.

Because your body doesn't just hold your story. It *is* your story.

Reflection Prompts

1 Where in my body do I feel the effects of stress, fatigue, or creative resistance the most?

2 What helps me return to balance — movement, rest, nature, or silence?

3 How does my energy fluctuate throughout the day, and how might I align my creative work with those natural rhythms?

4 What small ritual can I create to honor my body before I write — a stretch, a breath, or a moment of sunlight?

CHAPTER 7
WRITING THROUGH
THE MIND
HOW TO KEEP YOUR NERVOUS
SYSTEM CALM ENOUGH TO CREATE

FROM BODY TO MIND

Once I began writing through the body — listening to its messages, honoring its cycles, and restoring its energy — my relationship with creativity changed completely.

But there was another layer waiting to be understood: the mind itself. If the body is the instrument, the mind is the frequency it tunes to.

Even when my body was nourished and rested, my thoughts could still spiral into overwhelm, self-criticism, or perfectionism. I realized that to write freely, I needed not just a calm body, but a *regulated mind*.

That became the next phase of my practice — learning how to work *with* my brain instead of against it, especially with the unique rhythms of ADHD and the emotional intensity of PMDD.

Because creativity isn't born from force; it's born from safety. And safety begins in the nervous system — but it extends into the mind.

THE MIND AS A CHANNEL

When people think of writing, they often picture a mind hard at work — analyzing, structuring, editing, perfecting. But for me, writing began to heal only when I stopped forcing my mind to perform and started learning how to regulate it.

The healing writer's greatest tool isn't discipline — it's regulation.

A calm nervous system creates a safe space for creativity to unfold. When your brain is overloaded, anxious, or overstimulated, it's nearly impossible to access flow. But when your body feels safe and your mind feels supported, the ideas come effortlessly — sometimes so clearly it feels like they were waiting for you all along.

Writing, I've learned, is not something we *do* to the mind; it's something that flows *through* it when we work with it, not against it.

THE ADHD BRAIN & CREATIVE FLOW

For much of my life, I thought something was wrong with me. I could hyperfocus for twelve hours straight one day and barely form a sentence the next. My ideas came in lightning bursts — brilliant but unpredictable. My mind was a kaleidoscope of thoughts, shifting faster than I could catch them. It wasn't until

I began learning about ADHD that I finally understood what was happening.

My brain isn't broken; it's simply wired for intensity.

That intensity can be my greatest creative gift — but only when I nurture the conditions it needs to thrive. I used to chase focus like it was a rare state that required caffeine, pressure, and chaos. Now I see that focus is a *feeling of safety.* My best writing doesn't come from adrenaline; it comes from coherence.

When dopamine and adrenaline are balanced — through proper nutrition, movement, and rest — my brain can drop into flow more easily. I no longer punish myself for the days when focus feels harder. I accept that creativity moves in waves. When I stop fighting those waves, I can surf them instead of drowning in them.

VAGUS NERVE & BREATHWORK

When I first understood how my ADHD brain worked, I realized that focus wasn't something I could force — it was something I could *feel into.* My most productive days weren't the ones where I pushed harder, but the ones where I felt calm, safe, and connected to my breath.

That's when I began to see the nervous system not just as biology, but as a creative instrument — one that could be tuned through breath, presence, and rhythm

When I first began writing at our local library **The House of Wisdom** — surrounded by stillness, sunlight, and the quiet hum of presence — I noticed something simple yet profound: the way I breathed determined how easily the words arrived.

When my breath was shallow, my thoughts scattered.

When I slowed it down, everything softened — my shoulders dropped, my mind cleared, and the writing flowed with ease.

That's when I began to understand the power of the **vagus nerve** — the body's internal bridge between mind and emotion.

The vagus nerve runs from the brainstem down through the heart and into the gut, influencing heart rate, digestion, and emotional regulation. It's what connects your inner world with your creative world.

When you breathe deeply and slowly, you stimulate this nerve, activating the **parasympathetic nervous system** — your body's "rest and create" mode. This is the opposite of the fight-or-flight response that so many of us write from: that anxious, perfectionist energy that keeps the body tense and the mind on high alert.

Now, before I begin writing — especially on days when my mind feels restless or overstimulated — I begin with a short breathing ritual. It's simple, but it changes everything.

My pre-writing breath practice:

- Inhale through the nose for **4 counts**.
- Hold gently for **7 counts**.
- Exhale slowly through the mouth for **8 counts**.
- Repeat **3–4 times**.

Sometimes I hum softly on the exhale — a low vibration that further activates the vagus nerve and deepens the sense of calm. Within minutes, I can feel my heartbeat steady, my nervous system settle, and my awareness expand.

That's when I know I'm ready to write — not from effort, but from coherence. **Breathing, I've learned, is the bridge between chaos and clarity**. It reminds your body that it's safe to create — and in safety, creativity blooms.

DIGITAL BOUNDARIES

If breathwork anchors my focus, boundaries protect it.

In the early drafts of *The Healing Journey*, I constantly interrupted myself — checking emails, scrolling, researching one more thing. It wasn't just distraction; it was a nervous system addicted to stimulation.

Our brains weren't designed to process the endless input of modern life. Every notification floods the system with microbursts of dopamine and cortisol — the same stress chemicals that drain focus and creativity. Over time, the mind begins to crave that external stimulation more than the quiet stillness creation requires.

Now, before I write, I put my phone in another room. I close all tabs except the one document I'm working on. I even light a candle — not for aesthetics, but as a signal to my brain that it's safe to enter deep focus.

At first, silence felt uncomfortable. My mind resisted it, reaching for the next distraction. But after a few weeks, something shifted. The silence became a sanctuary. My brain learned to crave stillness as much as it once craved noise.

Boundaries are not restrictions — they're protection for your creative life force.

JOURNALING AS MENTAL HYGIENE

Whenever my mind feels cluttered or self-critical (this happens often), journaling becomes my therapy. My hard copy A4 sized journal is where I offload the mental noise before I begin writing for others. I call it "mental hygiene" — the same way you'd shower before meeting someone, journaling cleanses the thoughts before you meet the page.

Some mornings, I fill a page with stream-of-consciousness writing: no editing, no judgment. Sometimes it's messy; sometimes it's profound. But it always creates space. Research by Dr. James Pennebaker has shown that expressive writing helps the brain reprocess emotion, improving both mental clarity and immune function.

For me, it's more than data — it's personal truth. Journaling helps me metabolize the emotions I'd otherwise carry into my creative work. When I give my mind a place to speak freely, it quiets enough for the deeper wisdom to emerge.

COMMUNITY & THERAPY

As a writer, solitude is necessary — but isolation can be dangerous. During seasons of burnout and motherhood, I learned how essential human connection truly is. The creative process is deeply emotional, and without supportive relationships, it can easily become overwhelming.

Therapy became my grounding space. It gave me language for the emotions that used to live unnamed inside me. Sharing my truth out loud softened the pressure I placed on my writing to hold everything.

Community, too, has been medicine. Honest conversations with friends and other writers remind me that I'm not alone in the struggle. Our brains regulate through co-regulation — calm nervous systems attune to one another. Connection, quite literally, keeps us sane. Writing can be solitary, but healing rarely happens in isolation.

Reflection Prompts

1 What patterns of thought pull me out of flow most often?

2 How does my body feel when my mind is overstimulated?

3 What digital habits drain my focus or creativity?

4 What breathwork or mindfulness practice could help me transition into writing mode?

A regulated mind invites revelation. When you learn to calm the storm within, you create the conditions for insight to surface — not through force, but through presence. Your words don't need to be chased. They will arrive the moment your mind feels safe enough to receive them.

CHAPTER 8
WRITING IN SYNC WITH YOUR CYCLE

HOW HORMONAL RHYTHMS MIRROR CREATIVE RHYTHMS

Once I learned to calm my mind and find coherence in stillness, I began noticing something deeper — a rhythm beneath the regulation.

Some days my focus flowed effortlessly; other days, I felt inward, reflective, or emotionally raw. For a long time, I judged that fluctuation as inconsistency. But what I eventually discovered was that it wasn't inconsistency at all — it was my cycle speaking. **That realisation changed everything.**

For most of my life, I tried to force creativity into structure — neat boxes of productivity that matched the rhythm of the world around me. Deadlines. Calendars. Expectations. I learned that:

"Creativity doesn't follow a calendar — it follows rhythm, emotion, and flow, just like nature itself."

There is a rhythm that lives inside every woman — one that pulses through our hormones, energy, and moods. When we learn to honor that rhythm, rather than resist it, we stop writing from pressure and start creating from flow.

The feminine creative cycle mirrors nature — not the corporate clock. Like the tides, the seasons, and the lunar phases, we move through our own inner seasons each month.

Once I began mapping my creative process onto my hormonal cycle, everything shifted. My writer's block softened. My self-judgment eased. I finally understood that there were days to bloom and days to rest — and that both were sacred.

Your cycle is not an inconvenience to work around.

It's a creative rhythm to work *with*.

THE FOUR CREATIVE SEASONS

1. Menstrual Phase — The Winter of Creativity (Days 1–5)

Rest, reflection, and intuitive vision.

During menstruation, hormones like estrogen and progesterone drop to their lowest point. The body is releasing, detoxifying, and renewing. It's a time to withdraw inward, to rest, to listen.

In creativity, this is your winter — the stillness before rebirth. The analytical mind quiets, and intuitive insight rises.

I often find this phase to be my most spiritually potent. The words that come here are softer, wiser, and more honest. This is not the time to push forward; it's the time to turn inward.

Creative Focus: Reflect, journal, edit softly, dream.

Mood: Quiet, intuitive, emotional.

Rituals: Herbal tea, womb massage, journaling by candlelight.

Foods: Iron-rich meals (lentils, beets, red meat, spinach) to replenish blood and energy.

Ask yourself: *What am I ready to release? What wisdom is rising beneath the silence?*

2. FOLLICULAR PHASE — THE SPRING OF CREATIVITY (DAYS 6–14)

Inspiration, initiation, and new ideas.

As estrogen rises, energy and motivation return. You feel lighter, clearer, more confident. This is when your brain thrives on novelty and play — perfect for brainstorming, planning, and starting new creative projects.

This phase is often where I feel most "myself" — grounded yet open, focused yet optimistic. Science shows that rising estrogen boosts dopamine and enhances verbal fluency, memory, and creative problem-solving.[1]

Creative Focus: Outlining, ideation, new beginnings.

Mood: Energized, optimistic, curious.

Rituals: Movement, nature walks, vision boards, cold showers to awaken the senses.

Foods: Fresh, colorful meals — greens, berries, fermented foods — to support rising estrogen and liver detoxification.

Ask yourself: *What excites me right now? What am I ready to begin?*

3. OVULATORY PHASE — THE SUMMER OF CREATIVITY (DAYS 15–17)

Expression, communication, and visibility.

Estrogen and testosterone peak, bringing confidence, charisma, and clarity. You feel magnetic — your words flow easily, your ideas connect effortlessly. This is the time to speak, teach, share, and publish.

I often record meditations, podcasts, or video content during ovulation — when my voice feels alive and expressive. It's also the best time to collaborate, as estrogen supports social connection and empathy.

Creative Focus: Presentations, speaking, sharing your work publicly.

Mood: Outgoing, confident, social.

Rituals: Dance, cacao ceremonies, connecting with community.

Foods: Light, hydrating meals — fruit, vegetables, smoothies — to support metabolism and energy.

Ask yourself: *How can I use my voice to serve others? What message feels ready to be shared?*

4. LUTEAL PHASE — THE AUTUMN OF CREATIVITY (DAYS 18–28)

Refinement, depth, and introspection.

As progesterone rises and estrogen dips, the energy turns inward again. This phase is where intuition deepens, emotions intensify, and truth reveals itself. For many women — especially those with PMDD or sensitivity to hormonal shifts — this can be the most challenging season.

But it's also profoundly creative. This is when I write my most emotionally charged chapters — raw, vulnerable, and true. It's the phase for editing, refining, and completing what you've started.

Support your nervous system with grounding foods, magnesium, and self-compassion. Allow more rest, less pressure, and gentle structure.

This isn't regression; it's integration.

Creative Focus: Editing, completion, reflection.

Mood: Sensitive, intuitive, detail-oriented.

Rituals: Magnesium baths, journaling, decluttering, slow walks.

Foods: Warm, grounding meals — sweet potatoes, seeds, herbal teas.

Ask yourself: *What needs completion? What truth still wants to be spoken before I rest?*

ALIGNING DEADLINES TO YOUR NATURAL CYCLE

One of the most powerful shifts I made as a writer was planning my work *with* my hormones, not against them.

- I schedule brainstorming and project planning during the follicular phase.

- I record, teach, or do interviews during ovulation.
- I edit and organize during the luteal phase.
- I rest and reflect during menstruation.

Even if your life doesn't allow total flexibility, simply knowing your rhythm can soften your expectations. Instead of forcing output when your body craves rest, you can plan ahead — honoring the seasons that support your creativity most naturally.

When you write in sync with your body, you no longer fear inconsistency. You begin to trust your cyclical power.

CREATIVE JOURNALING PROMPTS BY PHASE

Menstrual (Winter)

- What am I releasing from this past cycle — in my body, life, or art?
- What wisdom is surfacing beneath my rest?

Follicular (Spring)

- What new ideas or projects feel alive in me?
- How can I bring more play into my creative process?

Ovulatory (Summer)

- How can I share my truth more boldly this week?
- What message or story feels ready to be seen?

Luteal (Autumn)

- What unfinished projects need closure?
- What emotions are asking to be expressed or witnessed?

When you write with your body, your art becomes alive. It breathes, moves, and changes with you — just as the moon moves through her phases and the earth through her seasons.

Your cycle is not your limitation. It is your creative compass. When you learn to honor it, you no longer chase inspiration — you *become* it.

CHAPTER 9
WRITING FOR LONGEVITY
HOW TO SUSTAIN CREATIVE OUTPUT WITHOUT DEPLETING YOURSELF

Once I began honoring my cyclical rhythm — writing with my body instead of against it — something deeper began to unfold. I realized that creativity isn't just seasonal; it's lifelong.

It's not about how much you create in a single phase, but how gently you sustain the flame through all of them.

That understanding became the foundation for the next chapter of my journey — learning how to write not just in flow, but for the long run.

When I first began writing, I thought consistency meant discipline — showing up every day, no matter what. I equated productivity with worth. If I didn't hit a word count, I felt guilty. If I took a day off, I felt behind.

But over time, especially after walking through adrenal fatigue and burnout, I learned a deeper truth: creative longevity has nothing to do with output and everything to do with *energy*.

As healing writers, we often carry the same perfectionism, over-responsibility, and emotional labor that once kept us safe. We pour our hearts into the page — and in the process, we risk depleting ourselves all over again.

Healing through writing means learning to create without recreating the same old burnout pattern. It means letting the process sustain you instead of drain you. It means remembering that your worth doesn't depend on how much you produce — but on how deeply you allow yourself to live, feel, and rest.

ENERGETIC HYGIENE: CLEARING EMOTIONAL RESIDUE

Writing about pain transforms it — but only if we also clear what it stirs up. After finishing a heavy chapter, I used to sit in emotional fog for hours, replaying memories that writing had unearthed. I thought that was part of the process. It was — but it wasn't meant to be permanent.

What I learned is that the emotions we access through writing need just as much care as the words we craft. Every time you revisit a difficult story, your nervous system relives fragments of that experience. If you don't consciously release the emotional charge afterward, you carry it into the next day's writing, the next relationship, the next project.

Now, I treat post-writing recovery as essential hygiene — just like brushing my teeth or washing my hands. After a deep writing session, I step outside, take three slow breaths, and let my body reset. I shake out my arms and legs, stretch my spine, drink water, or sit quietly in sunlight. Sometimes I listen to grounding music or journal a single sentence: *I've released this part of my story.*

These small rituals signal to my body that it's safe again — that the story has been witnessed, and I don't have to carry it anymore.

Healing writing is powerful — but integration is what makes it sustainable.

THE ART OF PAUSING

There's a myth in the creative world that stopping means losing momentum. But in truth, pausing is what *builds* momentum. It's the exhale that makes the next inhale possible.

When I wrote *The Healing Journey*, I began scheduling "non-writing days" into my calendar — not as failure, but as fuel. On those days, I'd walk barefoot on grass, spend time with my daughter, or simply sit in stillness. Inevitably, inspiration would return in ways that forced writing never could.

Rest is not the opposite of productivity. It's the soil that nourishes it.

In physiology, recovery isn't optional; it's the time when repair, growth, and integration happen. The same is true for creativity. If you never pause, your nervous system never leaves survival mode — and survival mode is the death of creativity.

Pausing is the art of letting life breathe between your words.

Earlier in 2025, I was introduced to the wisdom of Kabbalah — a mystical branch of Jewish spirituality that explores the laws of energy, creation, and divine consciousness. One of the teachings that deeply moved me was about rest. In Kabbalah, the Sabbath is seen as the day you hand everything over to the Creator — a sacred pause where you stop striving and allow divine energy to complete what you began. Instead of punishing myself for not working or not being productive, I started practicing this too: to let things rest, to hand over my work to the Creator, and to trust that it will grow into what it's meant to become.

That same principle applies to writing. After every creative cycle comes a sacred pause — a moment to hand over what's complete and let your body, mind, and nervous system reset.

NERVOUS SYSTEM CARE BETWEEN DRAFTS

The gap between finishing one draft and starting the next can feel like freefall. You've poured everything out, but the body is still catching up. This is where nervous system care becomes vital.

After finishing a draft, I often feel both exhilarated and empty — like my brain is buzzing but my soul is quiet. That's the time to shift from expression into replenishment. I focus on nourishment rather than output.

My post-draft ritual looks like this:

- **Nutrition:** grounding meals with protein, minerals, and healthy fats. Magnesium glycinate for muscle and nervous system relaxation.
- **Movement:** gentle yoga or walking instead of high-intensity workouts.

- **Nature:** sunlight, grounding, time outdoors to discharge mental energy.
- **Silence:** no podcasts, no multitasking, no input. Just stillness.
- **Reflection:** journaling gratitude for what was completed — not what's next.

Your nervous system is the container for your creativity. When it's calm, ideas have space to land. When it's overloaded, even genius feels like chaos.

Between drafts, care for the vessel that carries your voice.

YOUR CREATIVE ECOSYSTEM

Your creativity is a living ecosystem — a dynamic web connecting body, mind, hormones, emotions, and spirit. Each part influences the others. When one element becomes depleted, the whole system feels it.

> *If your body is undernourished, your brain can't focus.*
> *If your mind is overstimulated, your heart closes.*
> *If your hormones are out of sync, your energy feels inconsistent.*

But when you tend to all parts — physical, mental, and cyclical — creativity begins to regenerate naturally. Your art stops being an extraction of energy and becomes a circulation of it.

Writing, then, is no longer a task. It becomes a relationship —

between you and your body, your story, and the unseen intelligence that guides both.

That relationship will evolve through seasons: expansion and contraction, light and dark, output and rest. Sustainability doesn't mean staying in perpetual bloom. It means honoring your winters as much as your summers — knowing that both are part of the creative rhythm.

Writing is medicine — but so are movement, stillness, sleep, sunlight, and sound.

To create sustainably is to live cyclically — to give as much as you receive, to rest as much as you rise.

Your creative longevity isn't built by chasing inspiration; it's built by honoring your energy.

When you learn to write from overflow instead of depletion,

your words will carry not just wisdom — but wholeness.

Reflection Prompts

1 How do I know when I'm forcing instead of flowing?

2 What signals does my body send when I need rest or nourishment?

3 What ritual helps me clear emotional residue after writing something heavy?

PART FOUR
SHAPING YOUR STORY
FROM CHAOTIC NOTES TO A CLEAR, COHERENT MESSAGE

CHAPTER 10
FROM SCATTERED PAGES TO SOULFUL CHAPTERS
HOW TO TURN CHAOS INTO CHAPTERS WITHOUT KILLING THE MAGIC

THE ART OF INTUITIVE STRUCTURING

Every healing book begins in chaos. Scraps of notes. Late-night voice memos. Journal entries written through tears while your baby finally naps. Words you thought you'd never show anyone. **That's exactly how mine began.**

When I first started writing *The Healing Journey*, I was still deep in survival mode — living in a Dubai apartment surrounded by unpacked boxes, trying to regulate my nervous system between PMDD flare-ups, ADHD hyper-focus, and motherhood exhaustion.

There was no outline, no "plan." Just fragments: journal pages stained with magnesium spray, notes on my phone titled *"Why can't I slow down?"* and *"What if I'm not broken, just burned out?"*

At first, I thought the mess meant I wasn't ready. But over time, I realized the mess *was* the story. Your first draft isn't supposed to be organized — it's supposed to be *alive*.

The goal isn't to control the chaos. It's to listen to what it's trying to tell you. That's what I call **intuitive structuring** — allowing the story to reveal its own order before you impose one on it. When you learn to trust that process, you stop fighting the mess and start *mining it.*

THE "RIVER METHOD" OF STORYTELLING FLOW

Think of your book like a river. At the source is your *why* — the moment that cracked you open. For me, that source was the day I realized my ADHD wasn't a flaw, it was information.

The day I stopped trying to fix myself and started asking, ***What is my body trying to teach me?*** That realization became the headwaters of everything I've written since.

From there, your story flows through curves, bends, and unexpected depths — moments of resistance and revelation.

Here's how to use the **River Method** to turn chaos into clarity:

1. Identify Your Source (The Headwaters)

- Ask: *What experience started this transformation?*
- Mine began with adrenal collapse and a diagnosis that forced me to rewrite my relationship with my body.
- That's where your book begins — not necessarily in time, but in *truth*.

2. Follow the Current (The Flow)

- As I read through my notes, I noticed certain currents: control, burnout, emotional intensity, surrender.
- Those became the natural flow of my chapters. Do the same. Look for patterns or phrases that keep resurfacing.
- Your soul is already leaving breadcrumbs.

3. Name the Riverbanks (Boundaries)

- When I started writing about ADHD, I was tempted to include every health protocol, every genetic finding, every supplement that changed my life.
- But not everything belongs in this river. The riverbanks protect the reader — and you — from overwhelm.
- Define what your book is *not* about. Let simplicity become strength.

4. Find the Confluence (Integration)

- As my story unfolded, I realised it wasn't just about ADHD or PMDD. It was about nervous system healing, emotional regulation, and self-compassion.
- That's the confluence — where multiple streams of your life merge into a larger message.

5. Reach the Ocean (Resolution)

- A healing book doesn't need a "happily ever after."

- For me, it ended with peace — not because everything was fixed, but because I finally trusted myself.
- That's your ocean moment. The point where you can say, "I'm still healing, but I'm home within myself."

TURNING CHAOS INTO CLARITY WITHOUT LOSING THE SOUL

When I started shaping my manuscript, I made the mistake of organizing too soon. I built color-coded spreadsheets, tried to map chapters by theme — and completely froze. The truth is, my left brain wanted order before my heart was ready to release the story.

So I scrapped the spreadsheets and started again — this time, intuitively. Here's the process I followed (and still use today):

Step 1: Gather Everything

- I printed my journal pages, screenshots, and voice memo transcriptions — even the 3 a.m. notes written during PMDD insomnia.

Step 2: Color-Code or Highlight Themes

I sat on the floor with highlighters:

- yellow for moments of burnout,
- blue for surrender,
- pink for breakthroughs,
- green for peace or joy.

Patterns emerged like constellations. That's when I realized: my chaos already had coherence — I just had to see it.

Step 3: Group by Energy, Not Event

- Instead of writing "Chapter 3: 2019 – The Year I Fell Apart," I wrote "Chapter 3: When My Body Started Speaking Louder Than My Mind."

That shift from *timeline* to *transformation* made my story breathe again.

Step 4: Create Chapter Anchors

- Each chapter got a center of gravity — a line that held its message.

For example:

> *"The moment I stopped trying to heal and*
> *started listening."*
> *"Rest is not weakness. It's remembrance."*

Every time the structure felt heavy, I returned to those anchor lines.

Step 5: Let It Breathe

- When you read your draft aloud, listen for resistance. If a section feels forced, move it. If a part feels tender, pause.

Your body knows when your story is ready to flow.

THE SCIENCE BEHIND STORY FLOW

Neuroscience backs what writers have known intuitively for centuries: **storytelling organizes chaos.**

Psychologist Jerome Bruner described narrative as the way humans create coherence between memory, identity, and emotion.

When we tell our stories, the brain weaves fragmented experiences into a linear arc — transforming confusion into clarity.

Functional MRI studies show that stories activate multiple regions of the brain — not just language centers but sensory, emotional, and motor areas (Mar, 2011).

That's why readers *feel* your story in their bodies.

But here's the paradox: the more you try to force order too early, the less creative flow you access.

Rigid planning activates the brain's **executive control network**, while intuitive, emotional writing engages the **default mode network**, responsible for imagination and meaning-making (Beaty et al., 2016).

That's why intuitive structuring works so beautifully for healing authors: it honors both sides of the brain — emotion first, logic later.

When you trust the process, your brain — and your book — begin to integrate naturally.

KEEP THE SOUL, ADD THE SPINE

When I first printed my manuscript, I cried. Not because it was perfect — but because it was *me* on paper. Every imperfect sentence, every breath between lines, carried my evolution.

That's what I mean by **keeping the soul.** Your book's *soul* is the energy, the emotion, the heartbeat that readers will feel even between the words.

Your book's *spine* is the structure that allows it to stand tall and reach others. Without the soul, your writing becomes formulaic.

Without the spine, it collapses under its own weight. With both — it becomes art. Think of your structure as scaffolding for truth, not a cage for creativity. Let it support you — not silence you.

Reflection Prompt

Print three of your raw journal entries or notes.

Read them slowly and highlight the sentences that still make your body react — the ones that tighten your chest or make you tear up. Those are the emotional anchors of your book.

Ask yourself:

What lesson do these moments carry?

How might this help someone else feel less alone?

That's where your structure begins.

WORKSHEET 6 — RIVER MAP TEMPLATE

TO BE COMPLETED AFTER READING CHAPTER 10: FROM SCATTERED PAGES TO SOULFUL CHAPTERS

Your story is not a straight line — it's a river. Some stretches move swiftly, others pause and swirl before finding their way forward. Each bend has its purpose. Each still pool holds wisdom. This worksheet helps you see the flow of your story — from the first stirrings of transformation to the lessons that merge into purpose. **Let your intuition lead**. Don't force order; let the river show you its natural path.

✦ Step 1 — The Five Sections of Your Story River

Every story has a current. Use these five phases to map the emotional and structural flow of your book. Write freely in each section — words, fragments, or short sentences are enough.

River Phase	Guiding Prompts	Notes / Story Seeds
Headwaters	What moment started my transformation? What was life like before the shift began?	
Flow	What were the major turning points, breakdowns, or breakthroughs? What themes keep resurfacing through these moments?	
Riverbanks	Who or what supported me through this season? What boundaries protect my message and energy as I write about it?	
Confluence	Where do the lessons begin to merge? How did understanding, healing, or clarity start to take form?	
Ocean	Where does my story meet the reader's needs? What truth, insight, or invitation do I want to leave them with?	

✦ Step 2 — Discovering the Current

Now that you've written into each phase, look for patterns and threads. Ask yourself:

- What emotion or theme runs through my story from start to finish?
- How does this theme mirror the journey I want my reader to take?

The emotional current that carries my story is:

_____

(Examples: Resilience, Forgiveness, Surrender, Awakening, Reconnection, Self-Trust.)

This is your story's *heartbeat*. Every scene, reflection, and chapter should connect back to this current in some way.

✦ Step 3 — Visual Mapping (Optional)

On a separate page or in your notebook, sketch your river. Mark:

- The **source** (your beginning moment).
- The **currents** (key events or emotional shifts).
- The **riverbanks** (boundaries or supports).
- The **confluence** (where lessons merge).
- The **ocean** (the message you'll share with others).

You can draw, list, or use arrows — whatever helps you *see the flow.*

✦ Step 4 — Reflection Prompt

"Where does my story feel most alive, and where does it feel stuck?

What might those places be trying to teach me about flow, trust, and surrender?"

_____

_____

_____

_____

_____

✦ Closing Intention

"My story moves like water — sometimes still, sometimes rushing, always finding its way.

I trust that every turn and pause serves the shape of my healing."

Signature: _____

Date: _____

CHAPTER 11
THE EMOTIONAL WORK OF WRITING

Earlier, in *Writing Through the Mind*, we explored how regulation helps you enter a creative state. But what happens after you've written something raw — when your own words stir emotions you thought you'd outgrown? That's where the real emotional work of writing begins.

WHAT HAPPENS WHEN WRITING STIRS OLD WOUNDS

Writing your healing story will move things — in your body, your mind, and your nervous system.

Some days, it will feel liberating. Other days, it will feel like standing barefoot on broken glass. That doesn't mean you're doing it wrong. It means the work is *working*.

When you write about past pain, you're not just using words — you're reactivating the neural and emotional pathways connected to those memories.

Your heart rate may increase. Your throat may tighten. You might find yourself exhausted after writing only a few pages.

I've felt that too.

When I began writing *The Healing Journey*, I thought I was simply recounting my experiences.

But sometimes, as I described moments of rage during PMDD or the helplessness of postpartum depletion, I'd suddenly feel that same heat in my chest again — as if my body didn't know the moment had passed.

That's because, on a biological level, **your body doesn't differentiate between remembering and reliving**.

The same regions that light up during a traumatic experience — particularly the amygdala and insula — also activate when you recall it in detail (van der Kolk, 2014). In other words: when you write, your body remembers.

This is why writing a healing book requires just as much *self-regulation* as self-expression.

WHEN OLD WOUNDS SPEAK

Writing can bring long-buried memories to the surface — the things you've minimized, spiritualized, or simply forgotten because they were too painful to face.

Sometimes these memories don't return as thoughts. They return as sensations — a heaviness in your chest, a racing heart, a knot in your stomach.

Those sensations are your body's language. They're not trying to hurt you — they're trying to finish what was once interrupted.

When I wrote about burnout and adrenal collapse, I noticed that my writing sessions mirrored my old patterns of overwork.

I'd push myself to write late at night, fueled by tea and adrenaline, even when my body begged me to rest. That's when I realized:

I was *repeating* the very thing I was trying to heal.

So I stopped forcing productivity and started practicing presence. I began to see writing not as extraction, but as conversation. If my body tensed up, I'd pause. Breathe. Step outside. Sometimes the lesson wasn't in the words I was writing, but in *how* I was writing them.

That's when I understood:

> *Healing doesn't happen from telling the story. It happens from feeling safe enough to tell it.*

NERVOUS SYSTEM REGULATION FOR WRITERS

When you write about trauma or transformation, you're engaging your **autonomic nervous system** — the part responsible for fight, flight, freeze, or fawn.

If left unchecked, writing can push you into dysregulation — the very opposite of the healing you're trying to create.

Here are tools I use (and teach) to regulate while writing:

1. Breathe with Intention

- Use the 4–6 method: inhale for 4 counts, exhale for 6.
- Longer exhales stimulate the vagus nerve, signaling safety to the body (Porges, 2011).

2. Ground Through the Body

- Notice your feet. Feel the weight of your hips in the chair.
- If you're at your desk, press your palms flat on the surface and imagine roots growing downward.
- Grounding helps bring your awareness from memory (past) to presence (now).

3. Create a "Safe Word" for Pause

- If a scene or memory feels overwhelming, choose a cue — like the word *pause* — to stop writing and reconnect to your body.
- Trauma therapist Peter Levine calls this creating "pendulation" — moving between activation and safety so the body can integrate instead of re-traumatize (Levine, 2010).

4. Use Somatic Transitions

- Before and after writing, move your body.
- Shake your arms. Walk barefoot outside. Stretch your spine.

- Movement helps release any energy stirred by emotional writing.

5. Limit Exposure to Triggers

- Avoid re-reading deeply emotional sections repeatedly in one session.
- Edit later, when the body is calm. Writing is emotional exposure therapy — it works best when done in small, contained doses.

EMBODIMENT, GROUNDING, AND SELF-CARE WHILE CREATING

Your body is not a bystander in your creative process. It's your co-author. When I wrote *Return to the Heart*, I realized that my best writing came after embodiment practices — not after caffeine or deadlines.

Some mornings, I'd begin with five minutes of breathing, then place my hand on my heart and ask, *"What does my body want to say today?"*

Some days, the answer was silence. Some days, it was truth I'd been avoiding for years. You don't have to go digging for pain. You just need to stay open to what arises — and grounded enough to receive it.

The body speaks the language the soul remembers. When you learn to listen, your writing becomes translation — not invention.

Here are simple self-care practices to support embodiment and creativity:

Before Writing

- Set an intention: "I'm writing to heal, not to perform."
- Do one grounding activity (walk, breathwork, or journaling).
- Choose a safe, comforting environment — soft lighting, gentle music, maybe essential oils like lavender or frankincense.

During Writing

- Keep water nearby (hydration helps the nervous system stay balanced).
- Notice your posture and breathing.
- If emotion rises, pause. Place your hand on your heart and whisper, *"I'm safe now."*

After Writing

- Step away. Let the nervous system settle.
- Do something that signals completion — wash your hands, light incense, stretch, or go outside.
- Talk to someone supportive if something big surfaced.

Research on expressive writing confirms that self-care *during* and *after* writing enhances integration and reduces distress (Sloan & Marx, 2004). Your well-being is not a distraction from your writing — it's the foundation of it.

WHEN YOU NEED TO STEP AWAY

Sometimes, writing about trauma may bring up sensations or emotions that feel too big to manage alone. If this happens, it's okay — even wise — to pause and reach out for professional or peer support. Healing isn't linear. Neither is writing. There is no "behind" in this process.

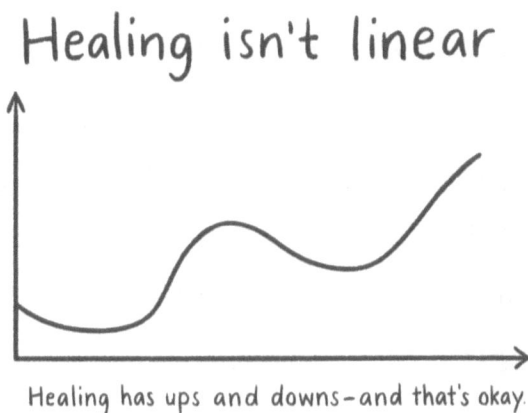

Healing has ups and downs–and that's okay.

You're not abandoning your book by taking care of yourself. You're modeling the very healing your story teaches.

WRITING AS INTEGRATION

Every time you regulate, breathe, and return to the page, you're teaching your body a new language: safety through expression.

Writing isn't just the story of your healing — it *is* the healing.

Each sentence is a small recalibration of your nervous system, proof that you can touch what once hurt and remain whole.

So when the emotions rise, let them.

The page is strong enough to hold them, and so are you.

Reflection Prompt

Think of a moment in your writing that felt physically or emotionally heavy.

What sensations did you feel in your body?

What might those sensations be asking for — rest, acknowledgment, release?

Then write a few lines that begin with:

"Even as I feel this, I know I am safe now."

WORKSHEET 7 — BODY CHECK & REGULATION LOG

TO BE COMPLETED AFTER READING CHAPTER 11: THE EMOTIONAL WORK OF WRITING

Writing a healing book isn't just a mental process — it's a *somatic one.* Every time you write, your body remembers. Sometimes that memory feels light and liberating; sometimes it feels heavy or tender.

This worksheet helps you track what's happening inside your body as you write, so you can recognize when you're expanding — and when you need to pause, ground, or care for yourself. You don't have to push through discomfort. You only have to stay present to it, with compassion.

✦ Step 1 — The Body Check-In

Before you write, take a few moments to notice how your body feels. No need to analyze — just observe.

Body Area / System	What I Notice Before Writing	What I Notice After Writing
Breath (shallow, deep, held?)		
Shoulders / Neck (tense, relaxed?)		
Jaw / Face		
Chest / Heart		
Stomach / Gut		
Hands / Posture		
Energy Level		
Overall Emotion		

Repeat this as often as you like — even a few times a week can reveal powerful patterns.

✦ Step 2 — Regulation Tools Menu

If you notice tension or emotional activation, choose one or two grounding practices from this list — or add your own.

Category	Examples	My Go-To Practices
Breath	4-7-8 breathing, box breath (4-4-4-4), sigh release	
Body	Stretch, shake out arms, gentle yoga pose, walk outside	
Sensory	Hold something textured, smell essential oils, sip warm tea	
Energy Reset	Cold water on wrists, hand on heart, 30 seconds of humming	
Connection	Message a trusted friend, cuddle a pet, pray or meditate	

The goal isn't to avoid emotion — it's to regulate your body so you can hold it safely.

✦ Step 3 — Recognizing Emotional Triggers

After each writing session, ask:

- What scene, topic, or phrase stirred the strongest emotion?
- Where did I feel that emotion in my body?
- What might it be trying to show me or release?

Write freely below:

_____

_____

_____

(Note: If deep grief, panic, or trauma responses surface, it's wise to pause and seek support — from a counselor, therapist, or trauma-informed guide.)

✦ Step 4 — The Regulation Log

Use this simple tracker to build awareness over time.

Date	Writing Focus / Scene	Emotion Level (1–10)	Grounding Used	How I Felt After

Patterns may emerge — maybe writing in the morning feels calmer, or certain topics need shorter sessions.

Self-awareness is self-care.

✦ Step 5 — Reflection Prompt

"What sensations or emotions tell me I'm reaching my edge — and how can I honor those signals instead of pushing past them?"

_____

_____

_____

_____

_____

✦ Closing Intention

"My body is part of my creative process.

I listen, I adjust, I care for it as I would a dear friend.

My nervous system doesn't slow my writing — it sustains it."

Signature: _____

Date: _____

CHAPTER 12
EDITING MADE SIMPLE
HOW TO POLISH YOUR BOOK WITHOUT LOSING THE MAGIC

B y the time you've written something that has truly moved you — maybe even undone you — you've already done the deepest work. But healing through writing doesn't end when the first draft is finished. That's only the beginning of integration.

Editing is where your story settles. It's where reflection becomes rhythm, and truth becomes art.

When I finished writing the first draft of *The Healing Journey*, I thought I was done. But when I printed it and held it in my hands, I could *feel* that it wasn't ready yet.

Something in me knew there were words that needed space to breathe, sentences that needed softening, and stories that needed time to settle before they were truly ready to be shared.

That's what editing really is — the integration phase. It's where you shift from the person *who lived the story* to the person *who's ready to share it.*

When you edit, you're not fixing your book. You're refining its medicine.

Editing, in many ways, is the quiet continuation of your healing. It's where the fire of creation cools into form — where emotion becomes meaning, and chaos turns into coherence. Think of this stage not as correction, but as communion with your story. You've already lived it; now you're shaping the energy it leaves behind.

To help you move through this phase with clarity and calm, here's an overview of the seven steps I use and teach — a simple guide to bring your book from raw draft to refined truth.

Editing at a Glance: The Seven Steps of Integration		
Step	Focus	Core Intention
1. Rest Before You Revise	Step away from your draft	Create distance so you can return with fresh eyes and emotional clarity.
2. Read Like a Reader	Reconnect with your story	Experience your book as your reader would; notice where energy rises or dips.
3. Shape the Flow	Refine the structure	Ensure each chapter serves a purpose and the emotional arc feels cohesive and alive.
4. Keep It Simple, Keep It You	Reclaim your authentic voice	Let your writing sound like you — warm, human, and real.
5. Cut What No Longer Serves	Edit with compassion	Release what was written for your healing, and keep what serves the reader's transformation.
6. Proof and Polish (Without Perfectionism)	Bring everything into harmony	Polish details without erasing your essence. Clarity matters more than perfection.
7. Know When It's Done	Surrender the outcome	Trust that your book now belongs to the readers who need it most.

STEP 1: REST BEFORE YOU REVISE

After finishing a draft, the best thing you can do is *walk away from it.*

When I finished *Thriving Naturally with ADHD*, I took two full weeks off from writing. I spent time in nature, drank cacao in the mornings, and didn't open the document once. When I finally did, I saw things I couldn't see before — the parts that flowed effortlessly, and the ones that felt a little heavy or forced.

That pause wasn't laziness — it was clarity in disguise. Your subconscious keeps working even when you're not. So give yourself space to reset. When you come back, you'll see your story through new eyes — not as the woman who *lived* it, but as the one who *learned* from it.

STEP 2: READ LIKE A READER

Before you start editing, read your book as if it wasn't yours.

Print it if you can — the energy of paper is different from a screen.

I always make a cup of tea, sit somewhere quiet, and read my book from start to finish without changing anything.

I circle or underline where the energy dips, where I feel confused, or where I can sense my nervous system tightening (that's usually a sign I'm not ready to share that part yet).

You'll notice where your reader might lose track, where your story gets tangled, or where a few lines of reflection could help anchor your truth.

STEP 3: SHAPE THE FLOW

Once you've read through it, look at your book as a whole.

Ask yourself:

- Does each chapter have a clear purpose or emotional takeaway?
- Does the story build naturally — from breakdown to breakthrough?
- Are there chapters that feel out of place or say the same thing twice?

For *Write It Anyway*, I created what I call a "chapter map."

I wrote each chapter title on a sticky note and laid them all out on the floor. Then I moved them around until the flow felt right — not logical, but *energetically right*.

When you see your book that way, it starts to feel like a living, breathing journey rather than just a sequence of pages.

STEP 4: KEEP IT SIMPLE, KEEP IT YOU

When I first edited *Return to the Heart*, I tried to sound like all the authors I admired — articulate, polished, perfect.

But every time I reread it, it didn't sound like me. So I went back and rewrote it in the tone I use when I talk to my coaching clients — warm, conversational, real.

If you're wondering whether something sounds right, read it aloud. If you wouldn't say it that way in real life, change it.

Your reader doesn't need perfect grammar — they need *you*.

STEP 5: CUT WHAT NO LONGER SERVES

This one's hard, especially when you're writing about healing. Every paragraph feels sacred.

But here's a truth I've learned: not everything you write is meant for the reader.

Some parts were meant to heal *you.* Others are meant to help *them.*

When I edited the chapter on PMDD rage in *The Healing Journey*, my first draft was too raw. It was still bleeding. I could feel my whole body tighten reading it back. So I cut it. Not because it wasn't true — but because I wasn't ready.

I came back to it months later, after I'd done the deeper inner work, and rewrote it from a calmer place. That's the version that made it into the book — not as a cry for help, but as a hand reaching out.

If it serves your message, it stays. If it only serves your memory, it goes. When in doubt, create a "Maybe" folder instead of deleting. You can always return later.

STEP 6: PROOF AND POLISH (WITHOUT PERFECTIONISM)

Once your book flows well, give it one last loving tidy-up.

Check for:

- Typos and repeated words
- Consistent tone and tense
- Spacing and headings that look clean on the page

You can use Grammarly or ProWritingAid for small errors, but don't over-polish your personality out of it. Your reader wants your voice, not a robot's.

Before sending *Write It Anyway* to print, I did a "final read on paper" — and yes, I caught things I never noticed on screen. Like extra spaces, uneven formatting, and even a missing period that changed the tone of an entire paragraph.

STEP 7: KNOW WHEN IT'S DONE

You'll never feel *completely* ready to let it go. I didn't.

Even after four proof prints of *The Healing Journey*, I found something small to tweak every time. But eventually, you realize the book doesn't belong to you anymore — it belongs to the people who need it. **The moment you stop editing for perfection and start editing for clarity, you're done**.

OPTIONAL: THE SACRED READ-THROUGH

Before I publish, I always do a quiet "ritual read." I light a candle, whisper a little prayer, and read the dedication out loud.

For *Thriving Naturally with ADHD*, I ended my final edit by saying, "It's safe to be seen."

That's when I knew it was ready. Because it wasn't just my book anymore. It was my offering.

THE HEART OF IT ALL

Editing isn't about being an expert. It's about becoming honest.

You're not fixing your story — you're finding its true rhythm.

You're not erasing the rawness — you're shaping it so it can reach others.

The version of you who's editing is wiser than the one who wrote the first draft.

Trust her.

She knows what stays, what goes, and when it's time to finally let the book go out into the world.

Reflection Prompt

As you move from creation into refinement, ask yourself:

What part of me is ready to release control — and what part still needs to rest?

Remember, your story doesn't need perfection.

It just needs peace.

WORKSHEET 8 — EDITING COMPASS

TO BE COMPLETED AFTER READING CHAPTER 12: EDITING MADE SIMPLE

Editing is not about perfection — it's about clarity and connection. It's where your story evolves from a personal expression into something that can hold space for others. When you edit consciously, you're not just revising your words — you're refining your energy, your focus, and your message.

This worksheet will help you edit with both precision and compassion, staying aligned with your truth as you polish your book for the world.

✦ Step 1 — Before You Begin: Ground and Reflect

Before opening your manuscript, take a moment to center yourself.

1. Close your eyes.
2. Inhale deeply, exhale slowly.
3. Place your hand on your heart and whisper:
   - "I can refine my story without losing its soul."

Now answer these quick check-in questions:

- What is my intention for this editing round? (e.g., clarity, flow, emotion, trimming length)

_____

_____

- How do I want to feel while editing? (calm, curious, creative, confident)

_____

_____

- What part of me needs compassion during this process?

_____

_____

✦ Step 2 — The Three Layers of Editing

Editing happens in layers. Don't try to do them all at once. Work through them gently, one at a time.

- **Layer 1 — Structure & Flow (Macro Edit):**
  - Look at the big picture. Does your book flow naturally? Does each chapter have a clear message and transformation?
- **Layer 2 — Voice & Clarity (Micro Edit):**
  - Focus on tone, rhythm, and readability. Does it sound like you? Are you saying what you mean with simplicity and truth?
- **Layer 3 — Language & Layout (Proofing):**
  - Tidy up spelling, grammar, formatting, and consistency. Read it aloud to catch anything that doesn't sound right.

(Tip: Leave at least 24 hours between each editing layer. It keeps your brain fresh and your perspective objective.)

✦ Step 3 — The Editing Compass

Use the compass below to make mindful decisions about what to **Keep**, **Cut**, **Clarify**, or **Combine.** This prevents emotional overwhelm and ensures no insight is lost.

Keep (Essential or Powerful)

_____

_____

Cut (No Longer Needed)

_____

_____

_____

_____

Clarify (Unclear or Repetitive)

_____

_____

Combine (Similar Ideas)

_____

_____

(Tip: Move cut sections into a "Maybe File." Sometimes pieces that don't belong in this book will become seeds for your next one.)

Step 4 — Emotional Safety Check

Editing a healing book can reawaken old emotions.

Pause if you notice tension, fatigue, or inner criticism surfacing.

Ask yourself:

- Is this discomfort coming from truth (something that needs to change) or from fear (self-doubt, perfectionism)?
- How can I bring compassion to this part of the process?

If needed, use one of your grounding tools from Worksheet 7 — *Body Check & Regulation Log* before returning.

Step 5 — The Integration Reflection

Once you've completed your current round of edits, reflect on what has changed — not just in your writing, but in you.

"How has refining my story deepened my understanding of myself?"

_____

_____

_____

_____

"What feels more clear, strong, or true now than when I began?"

_____

_____

_____

_____

_____

Step 6 — Closing Intention

When your editing session is complete, whisper this simple mantra to close the loop:

"My words are whole. My story is clear.

I can let this version live and breathe."

Signature: _____

Date: _____

CHAPTER 13
HOW TO USE AI AS A CREATIVE PARTNER

FROM ARTIFICIAL INSEMINATION TO ARTIFICIAL INTELLIGENCE

W hen I first heard the term "AI," I wasn't thinking about robots or algorithms — I was thinking about dogs and horses.

Back in 2006, while living in the Netherlands, I modeled for a photoshoot at **Stal Eurocommerce**, a prestigious Dutch showjumping stable in Lunteren, Gelderland. After the shoot, we were each gifted a beautiful coffee-table book about the showjumping stud. As I flipped through its glossy pages, I noticed photos of tiny frozen straws and, curious, asked what they were. Someone explained they were used for **artificial insemination** — my first introduction to "AI," though in a very different context.

Fast-forward to 2010, when I was working on a German sport horse stud in Queensland, Australia. The property bred high-performance showjumping horses, and I was there to complete my 90 days of regional work — a requirement for my second working holiday visa. It was there that I witnessed my first equine AI procedure in real life. I'll spare you the details (let's just say it was memorable), but back then, AI had nothing to do with computers and everything to do with creating life.

Now, years later, I find myself in a completely different chapter of life — using that same abbreviation in a whole new way. This time, **AI** stands for *artificial intelligence* — or as some in the spiritual community like to say, *advanced intelligence.* And in a way, that feels true. Because when used consciously, AI isn't just a tool of logic; it's a bridge between creativity and consciousness. It's a technology that, like any form of creation, reflects the energy of the one using it.

For many people, the idea of blending art, healing, and artificial intelligence might feel strange — even wrong. I understand that resistance. For a long time, I worried that using AI would make my writing less authentic, less "me." But over time, I realized that technology doesn't replace our humanity; it mirrors it. Just as editing helps refine your voice without erasing your truth, AI can help amplify your creative process when used with clear intention.

Artificial Intelligence isn't good or bad — it's neutral. It becomes powerful only through the consciousness guiding it. If you bring fear or resistance, it will feel mechanical. But if you bring heart, clarity, and purpose, it can become one of your most valuable creative allies. In health and wellness, AI is already supporting breakthroughs in genetics, nutrition, and neuroscience. In writing and publishing, it can help you brainstorm ideas, organize your structure, refine your tone, and free up more time for what truly matters — *the soul work.*

The truth is, we're entering a new era of conscious creation. The goal isn't to let AI write for you — it's to let it write *with* you. To use it as a creative companion, not a replacement.

So, as we step into this chapter, think of AI as a quiet, reliable assistant — a tool that helps bring your ideas into form while you stay anchored in your own authenticity and purpose. Because whether we're talking about artificial insemination or artificial intelligence, creation in any form always comes down to one thing: **intention.**

Now that we've cleared up what kind of AI we're really talking about — let's explore how this new kind of intelligence can become a powerful ally in your creative journey. You don't need to be a tech expert or data analyst to use it. You simply need the same qualities that every conscious creator brings to the page: curiosity, awareness, and heart.

USING AI AS YOUR CREATIVE ASSISTANT (NOT YOUR REPLACEMENT)

Technology doesn't have to take away your creativity — it can help you *expand* it.

When used with discernment, AI becomes less of a machine and more of a mirror — a reflection of your ideas, your energy, and your intention. It's there to serve your creative flow, not to replace your voice.

Think of it as the assistant who never gets tired, never judges your half-finished drafts, and patiently waits for direction. It can help you brainstorm chapter titles, organize your thoughts, or polish your language when your mind feels scattered. But it can't feel what you feel — and that's exactly where your magic lies.

When I use AI, I don't see it as outsourcing creativity. I see it as *holding space* for it. The same way a yoga mat supports your body or a journal holds your emotions, AI holds your ideas until you're ready to shape them. It helps you stay organized, inspired, and efficient — without ever crossing the line into authorship.

The key is to stay anchored in your own creative authority.

AI can echo your tone, refine your rhythm, and even challenge you to think in new ways, but only you can breathe soul into the words. Only you can turn experience into wisdom.

Used consciously, AI becomes part of your ritual — a bridge between structure and spirit.

It's not here to write for you. It's here to help you write *from* a place of clarity, flow, and embodied truth.

THE MINDSET SHIFT: FROM RESISTANCE TO RELATIONSHIP

For many writers, the idea of using AI feels uncomfortable — even threatening. It can trigger the same resistance that arises when we try something unfamiliar in our creative or healing process. You might wonder, *"Will it make my work less authentic?"* or *"Does using AI mean I'm not a real writer?"*

But authenticity has never been about who (or what) types the words. It's about where those words come from — the energy behind them, the emotion that shapes them, and the truth that only *you* can express.

The truth is, every author has always had help. Editors, proofreaders, researchers, coaches — even the people we talk to over coffee who inspire a single line in our story. AI is simply a new kind of helper — faster, yes, but still dependent on your direction, your discernment, and your heart.

The shift happens when you stop seeing AI as a replacement and start seeing it as a relationship. Like any collaboration, it requires boundaries and trust. You don't hand it your soul work and walk away — you invite it to assist with the structure, the systems, and the details that allow your creativity to breathe.

When used with integrity, AI can help you stay connected to what truly matters — the message, not the mechanics. It can lighten your cognitive load, giving you more mental space to be intuitive, embodied, and present with your story.

So instead of resisting it, try this:

Ask how AI can *support* your humanity, not replace it.

How it can make your process smoother, not shallower. And how it can help you bring more of yourself — not less — to the page. Because the goal isn't to automate creativity.

It's to deepen your relationship with it.

WHAT AI CAN (AND CAN'T) DO

When used consciously, AI becomes a bridge between inspiration and execution. It can organize chaos into clarity, transform scattered notes into flow, and help you bring form to ideas that have been floating in your mind for months.

But like any tool, it has limits — and understanding those limits is where your creative power stays intact.

Here's what AI *can* do for you:

- Help you brainstorm fresh titles, subheadings, or chapter structures when you're too close to your work to see it clearly.
- Summarise long transcripts, interviews, or research papers so you can focus on the essence, not the overwhelm.
- Reorganise your notes into a clear narrative arc or logical flow.
- Polish grammar, transitions, and readability — without altering your message.
- Generate lists, prompts, or checklists that make your book more interactive and reader-friendly.
- Assist with crafting marketing copy — such as book descriptions, blurbs, or author bios — while you ensure they still sound like *you.*

And here's what AI *cannot* (and should never) do:

- Tell your story. It wasn't there — you were.
- Feel the heartbreak, the breakthroughs, or the divine timing behind your words.
- Replace your creative intuition, emotional truth, or embodied wisdom.

- Decide what's sacred, what's personal, or what belongs to your reader's journey.

AI is neutral — neither savior nor threat. It becomes meaningful only through the consciousness of the person using it. When guided by awareness, it can hold the structure, freeing you to focus on the soul.

The magic happens not in what AI produces, but in what *you* bring to it — your voice, your vision, your vibration. That's what makes your writing human, healing, and whole.

ETHICAL COLLABORATION: MAINTAINING YOUR VOICE AND INTEGRITY

Working with AI is like co-creating with a very capable assistant — one that never sleeps, never judges, and never truly *feels*.

That's why integrity matters more than ever.

The moment we invite technology into something as sacred as storytelling, we also take on the responsibility to use it consciously.

AI is best used when it enhances your creative process — not when it shortcuts your healing or replaces your embodied truth. Your words carry lived energy, memory, and emotion; AI can support their delivery, but it can't source their soul.

Here are a few guiding principles for ethical, heart-led collaboration:

1. Keep the Human in the Loop

- Never let AI be the final voice. Everything it helps you generate should pass through your nervous system, your intuition, and your truth before it reaches your reader. Ask yourself: *Does this feel aligned in my body?* If not, edit until it does.

2. Write First — Edit with AI Later

- Let your first drafts be wild, emotional, unfiltered. Write with your whole heart — not a machine in mind. Then, once the essence is alive on the page, invite AI to refine, structure, or polish. Healing stories are written in rhythm with your body, not a processor's logic.

3. Support, Don't Substitute

- It's fine to use AI for outlines, summaries, or research — but not for storytelling, empathy, or emotional nuance. Those belong to you. AI can *simulate* emotion, but only you can embody it.

4. Protect Privacy and Sacredness

- Never upload raw or sensitive material — especially personal trauma stories or client case studies — into public AI systems. Paraphrase or anonymize instead. Remember: your story is sacred, and privacy is a form of respect.

5. Be Transparent (If You Choose)

- If AI supported parts of your process — such as summarizing notes or editing — it's okay to mention it. Readers appreciate honesty, and your openness models what ethical creativity looks like in this new age.

When used with integrity, AI becomes a tool of empowerment, not dilution. It allows you to stay anchored in what matters — your message, your embodiment, your intention — while lightening the mental load of the creative process.

The goal isn't perfection; it's presence. AI can refine your words, but only you can infuse them with life.

HOW I USE AI IN MY OWN WRITING

When I write, I treat AI the same way I treat my journal, my cacao ritual, or my candle before a creative session — as a **companion**, not a crutch.

It's not there to do the work for me. It's there to hold space for the work to unfold.

I begin every project by writing freely — stream-of-consciousness style — letting emotion and intuition lead. Only after the essence has been expressed do I invite AI in to support the structure.

For me, it's like working with a quiet creative partner who's always available to brainstorm, organize, or polish, without ever losing patience.

Here are a few ways I use it in my own process:

- **To organise notes and patterns:** I often upload my raw journal entries, voice notes, or mind maps and ask AI to cluster ideas into themes — like *healing*, *ADHD clarity*, *motherhood*, or *purpose*. This helps me see how threads connect across chapters.
- **To summarise research:** When I'm reading scientific papers or health journals, I'll ask AI to distill complex ideas into plain language — then I rewrite it in my own voice so it feels warm and human.
- **To refine tone and consistency:** Before final editing, I might ask, *"Does this chapter feel cohesive in voice and rhythm?"* It helps me spot sections where I've drifted into lecture mode instead of storytelling.
- **To stay productive during low-energy days:** Some days, especially during my luteal phase, focus feels harder. Using AI for structure or outlining helps me keep momentum without burnout.

Every paragraph, every story, every reflection still comes from lived experience. No machine can replicate embodiment.

POPULAR AI TOOLS

If you're new to this world, start simple. These are tools I personally use and recommend — each with its own strengths depending on what part of the writing process you're in:

- **ChatGPT or Claude** — Best for brainstorming, outlining, tone feedback, and big-picture idea organization.

- o *Try this:* "Help me organize my book about emotional healing into a clear, three-part structure that moves from breakdown to breakthrough." (for more prompt ideas refer to Appendix B)
- **Grammarly or ProWritingAid** — Great for grammar, readability, and flow. Use them at the polishing stage, not the creative one. Think of them as digital proofreaders, not editors.
- **Notion AI or ClickUp AI** — Helpful for project management and note organization. You can store your book outline, research references, or daily writing schedule in one place.
- **Perplexity.ai or Elicit.org** — Designed for research. These platforms find credible sources, studies, and data faster than traditional search engines, which is ideal for evidence-based or science-backed writing.
- **Sudowrite or Jasper** — More creative AI tools that can assist with story flow, sensory description, or brainstorming metaphors. I only use them after I've written my first draft to see if they inspire new language — never as replacements.

Mindful Use Tip: Always cross-check facts, never share sensitive information, and keep your raw emotional writing offline. Use AI as a filter for clarity, not as a vault for your story.

All of these tools are available online — most offer free versions or trials. Start with one that feels intuitive rather than overwhelming. You don't need them all; you just need one that complements your creative rhythm.

A good rule of thumb: *If it helps you create with more clarity and peace, it's aligned. If it pulls you out of presence, it's noise.*

AI can be a brilliant support system when used consciously. It helps you stay organized, inspired, and efficient — but it's your lived experience, your heart, and your healing that give your book its power.

When you use technology to serve your vision — not shape it — you create something timeless.

Reflection Prompt

Before you create, ask yourself:

Am I using this tool with fear or with faith?

Technology becomes sacred when guided by intention —

what matters most is the energy behind your creation.

WORKSHEET 9 — ETHICAL AI PROMPTS LIBRARY

TO BE COMPLETED AFTER READING CHAPTER 13: HOW TO USE AI AS A SELF-PUBLISHING AUTHOR

AI can be a creative ally — but only when guided by your wisdom. Used consciously, it can help you organize thoughts, clarify structure, and research efficiently.

Used carelessly, it can dilute your voice and disconnect you from the truth that only you can tell.

This worksheet helps you collaborate with AI ethically — so your story remains human, heartfelt, and healing.

✦ Step 1 — Clarify Your Boundaries Before You Begin

Reflect before opening any AI tool. Write down what parts of your creative process you want to protect.

Creative Element	Keep 100% Human	Open to AI Support	Notes
Core story & emotional truth	✓		My lived experience only
Structural organization		✓	Outline, chapter flow
Grammar & readability check		✓	Light touch only
Tone or rewriting	✓		Maintain authenticity
Research or citations		✓	Fact-checking & summaries

Notes:

_____

_____

_____

_____

_____

Mantra:

"AI supports my process; it does not define my voice."

✦ Step 2 — Try These Soul-Aligned Prompt Templates

Use these prompts as gentle starting points. Adapt them to your story's tone and message.

(Tip: Always review and rewrite outputs in your own words before using them.)

1. **Chapter Clarity Prompt**

"Help me outline a chapter about [theme] using the flow: story → lesson → invitation.

I want to keep the tone warm, empowering, and authentic."

2. **Reflection Refinement Prompt**

"Summarize this paragraph clearly while preserving emotional depth and compassion."

3. **Research & Resources Prompt**

"List 3–5 peer-reviewed sources or credible studies about [topic] in accessible language, suitable for a healing-focused nonfiction book."

4. **Tone Alignment Prompt**

"Rewrite this paragraph so it sounds like my natural speaking voice — calm, grounded, encouraging."

5. **Brainstorming Prompt**

"Suggest creative titles or section headings for a book about [core theme], written by a [describe yourself briefly].

Keep them simple, soulful, and inspiring."

6. **Sensitivity Prompt**

"I'm writing about trauma and healing. Suggest ways to phrase this scene with emotional safety and compassion."

✦ Step 3 — My Personal Prompt Notes

As you experiment, use this space to record what works best for you.

Prompt I Tried	What Worked Well	What I Changed to Sound Like Me

_____

_____

_____

_____

_____

✦ Step 4 — Voice Integrity Check

Before including any AI-assisted text in your book, pause and ask yourself:

- Does this sound like me — or like a machine?
- Do these words still carry my emotional truth?
- Does this align with the ethical intention of my story?

If the answer isn't a full-body "yes," rewrite it.

Your reader is here for *you,* not an algorithm.

✦ Step 5 — Reflection Prompt

"Where does AI make my process easier — and where might it tempt me to bypass my own intuition?"

_____

_____

_____

_____

_____

PART FIVE
GETTING IT OUT INTO THE WORLD

PRACTICAL STEPS TO PUBLISH, SHARE, AND PROTECT YOUR ENERGY

CHAPTER 14

TRADITIONAL VS. SELF-PUBLISHING

CHOOSING HOW TO SHARE YOUR STORY WITH THE WORLD

E very book has two births — the first when it's written, and the second when it's shared.

When I finished writing *The Healing Journey*, I thought the hardest part was over. But then came the question that every author eventually faces: *How will I share this with the world?*

At first, I thought there was only one "real" way — traditional publishing. I pictured holding a hardcover with a major logo on the spine, my book on bookstore shelves, proof that I had "made it."

But the more I researched, the more uneasy I felt. The waiting lists, the query letters, the rejections, the loss of creative control — something in me resisted.

It wasn't about impatience. It was about intuition.

I didn't want to ask for permission to share my own story. I wanted ownership. I wanted to hold my book in my hands, not years later, but now — raw, real, imperfect, and alive.

So I chose the independent path.

I remember sitting at my laptop late one night, my toddler asleep beside me, my heart pounding as I uploaded *The Healing Journey* to Amazon KDP. I triple-checked every file, every margin, every line. When I finally hit "Publish," I burst into tears.

It wasn't about validation — it was liberation.

By morning, my book was live around the world. No gatekeepers. No delays. Just me, my words, and the readers they were meant for.

That moment taught me that self-publishing isn't a fallback plan — it's an act of courage.

THE TWO PATHS TO PUBLICATION

When it comes to publishing, there's no single "right" choice. There are two main routes — **traditional publishing** and **self-publishing** — and both can be powerful, depending on your goals, timeline, and temperament.

Think of it like this:

- Traditional publishing is partnership.
- Self-publishing is ownership.

Each has its own rhythm, rewards, and trade-offs.

TRADITIONAL PUBLISHING: THE PROMISE AND THE PRICE

Traditional publishing can be deeply fulfilling if you value prestige, expert guidance, or seeing your book in major stores. But it's also a slower, more selective process that requires patience — and sometimes compromise. Here's what to expect:

1 You'll Likely Need a Literary Agent

- Agents act as gatekeepers to large publishers. They handle submissions and contracts, usually taking 15% of your earnings.

2 Timelines Are Long

- From proposal to publication, it can take 18 to 36 months. If you thrive on momentum or have a time-sensitive message, this delay can feel discouraging.

3 You May Lose Creative Control

- Publishers often change titles, covers, or even tone to suit market trends. For authors writing healing or deeply personal stories, that can feel like losing part of your truth.

4 Royalties Are Lower

- Most authors earn around 10–15% of the book's retail price — sometimes less for paperbacks.

5 Marketing Is Still on You

- Unless you're already well known, you'll be expected to promote your own book. The myth that publishers handle everything is, unfortunately, outdated.

Traditional publishing can be a beautiful path if you:

- Want mainstream distribution and bookstore visibility.
- Prefer having a professional team manage editing, design, and printing.
- Are willing to play the long game and accept shared creative control.

It's the path of partnership — structured, reputable, and steady.

SELF-PUBLISHING: THE PATH OF EMPOWERMENT

Self-publishing used to be seen as second best. Not anymore. Today, it's a thriving global movement — one built on creative freedom, speed, and sovereignty.

Here's why I believe it's the most empowering choice for healing authors and modern creators:

1 Creative Freedom

- You decide the title, tone, and timeline. No one edits out your truth to fit a trend. When I wrote *Thriving Naturally with ADHD*, I kept the parts that mattered most — even the messy, vulnerable moments. That honesty became my strength.

2 Speed and Flexibility

- You can release your book within weeks of finishing it, or take as long as you need. The timeline is entirely yours.

3 Ownership and Royalties

- Platforms like Amazon KDP and IngramSpark give you 60–70% of royalties per sale. You keep your rights, your files, and your future options — from audiobooks to courses.

4 Global Reach

- With print-on-demand, your book can be available in over 190 countries overnight, without storing a single copy.

5 Lifelong Leverage

- A self-published book can become the foundation for your business or mission. You can expand it into a workshop, an online course, a journal, or a keynote talk — all on your own terms.

Self-publishing isn't about doing everything yourself. It's about directing the process. You can hire editors, designers, and proofreaders — the same professionals that traditional publishers use — while maintaining full control of your message and brand. Here's a quick comparison:

Quick Comparison: Control, Royalties, and Reach		
Feature	Traditional Publishing	Self-Publishing
Timeline	18–36 months	1–3 months (your pace)
Royalties	10–15%	60–70%
Creative Control	Shared	100% yours
Rights Ownership	Publisher	You
Upfront Cost	None	You invest (editing, design, proof)
Marketing	Primarily author-led	Entirely author-led
Distribution	Bookstores & libraries	Global online retail

HOW TO CHOOSE WHAT'S RIGHT FOR YOU

Choosing your publishing path is both practical and energetic. **Ask yourself:**

- Do I want creative freedom or traditional recognition?
- Do I prefer independence or structured support?
- Is timing important, or am I comfortable waiting?
- How hands-on do I want to be with design, marketing, and production?

If your heart values autonomy, speed, and authenticity — self-publishing may feel like home. If you're drawn to prestige, partnership, and patience — traditional publishing may align better. Neither path is "better." One simply fits your season, your nervous system, and your purpose more naturally than the other.

FINAL REFLECTION

When I look back, I'm grateful I trusted my intuition.

Self-publishing didn't just give me a book — it gave me confidence, clarity, and creative sovereignty. Plus it gave me a wonderful new connection with IngramSpark and Lightning source who facilitated my first public speaking appearance.

Self publishing reminded me that waiting for permission is just another form of self-doubt.

Because at the end of the day, publishing your book isn't about the path you choose — it's about the courage it takes to say:

"My story matters, and it's ready to be shared."

Reflection Prompt

If fear, rejection, or waiting for approval weren't in the way — which path would you choose?

Write a letter to your future self explaining why that choice feels aligned with your energy, your story, and your purpose.

WORKSHEET 10 — PUBLISHING PATH CLARITY QUIZ

TO BE COMPLETED AFTER READING CHAPTER 14: TRADITIONAL VS. SELF-PUBLISHING

Publishing your healing story is more than a logistical decision — it's an energetic one. It's about how you want your book to live in the world, and how you want to feel in the process.

This quiz will help you get clear on which path aligns best with your personality, timeline, and vision: **Traditional Publishing** or **Self-Publishing.** There's no right answer — only what's right for you.

✦ Step 1 — What Matters Most to Me?

Circle or check whichever statement feels true for you.

Consideration	If You Choose Mostly A	If You Choose Mostly B
Creative Control	A. I'm happy to follow industry standards and let a team make final decisions.	B. I want full creative freedom over my message, design, and timing.
Timeline	A. I'm patient — even if it takes years to get published.	B. I'd rather move at my own pace and release when I'm ready.
Marketing	A. I prefer someone else to handle PR, though I'll still help promote.	B. I'm open to learning marketing or hiring my own team when needed.
Royalties	A. I'm okay with smaller royalties if it means broader distribution.	B. I value higher royalties and direct ownership, even if growth is gradual.
Validation	A. Having a publishing house's name on my book feels important.	B. I trust that my story's impact matters more than external validation.
Entrepreneurial Spirit	A. I'd rather focus on writing than the business side of publishing.	B. I enjoy learning new skills and treating my book like a creative business.
Flexibility	A. I'm fine with contracts and deadlines set by others.	B. I prefer to set my own schedule and make changes whenever I need.

✦ Step 2 — Tally Your Results

- **Mostly A's → Traditional Publishing may suit you.**

You value professional guidance, structure, and having a team handle logistics. You may enjoy the prestige of a publishing imprint and long-term distribution channels.

- **Mostly B's → Self-Publishing may align best.**

You value freedom, flexibility, and full ownership of your creative vision. You're willing to learn new skills, outsource help, and build your book as part of your body of work.

(If you're a mix, you might consider hybrid publishing or releasing your first book independently to build confidence.)

✦ Step 3 — Reflect on Your Lifestyle and Energy

Ask yourself:

- How much *time* do I realistically have for marketing and logistics?
- How comfortable am I with learning tech or outsourcing help?
- How important is speed versus external validation?
- What kind of publishing journey feels most *peaceful* to my nervous system?

Write your insights here:

_____

_____

_____

_____

_____

✦ Step 4 — Visualize Your Ideal Publishing Experience

Close your eyes for a moment and picture your book in the world — readers holding it, reading your story.

Ask yourself:

• What does that moment feel like?

• Who helped me bring it to life?

• What kind of publishing path allowed me to stay grounded and proud?

Then complete this sentence:

"My ideal publishing path feels _____, because it honors _____."

_____

_____

_____

_____

_____

✦ Step 5 — Core Takeaway Table

Use this quick reference to summarize your clarity:

Factor	Traditional	Self-Publishing	My Choice / Hybrid Idea
Creative Control	Publisher decides	You decide	
Royalties	5–15%	60–80%	
Timeline	1–3 years	3–6 months	
Upfront Cost	Low	Moderate (design, editing, setup)	
Long-Term Ownership	Publisher owns ISBN	You own all rights	
Marketing	Shared responsibility	100% your responsibility	

(Tip: Even if you self-publish, you can still seek traditional publishing later. Ownership gives you flexibility.)

✦ Step 6 — Reflection Prompt

"If I stopped worrying about what's 'impressive' and chose what feels empowering — which publishing path would I pick, and why?"

_____

_____

_____

_____

_____

CHAPTER 15
BECOMING YOUR OWN PUBLISHER

S elf-publishing isn't about "doing it alone." It's about taking full ownership of your story — the creative, energetic, and practical sides of bringing it into the world.

When you self-publish, you become not just an author, but a **publisher.**

That means you own your book as an *intellectual property asset* — something that can generate income, credibility, and impact for years to come.

This chapter gives you everything you need to publish your healing book from start to finish — confidently, professionally, and soulfully.

STEP 1: UNDERSTANDING ISBNS (YOUR BOOK'S ID NUMBER)

ISBN stands for *International Standard Book Number.*

It's a unique 13-digit code that identifies your book in bookstores, libraries, and databases.

Think of it as your book's digital fingerprint — it tells the world: *This work belongs to you.*

Why You Need an ISBN

- It registers your book as a legitimate publication.
- It allows you to sell in online and physical bookstores.
- It lets you track and manage sales data.
- It proves ownership and helps protect against plagiarism.

You Need a Separate ISBN For

- Each **format** of your book (eBook, paperback, hardcover, audiobook).
- Each **edition** (for example, a revised edition later on).
- Sometimes even each distribution platform.

When you self-publish, you are both the **author** and the **publisher**. But when you upload your book to different distributors (for example, Amazon KDP and IngramSpark), they each act as a separate printing and distribution system. Even if the book's content is identical, the ISBN also identifies the publisher of record — meaning that one ISBN cannot legally belong to two different distribution entities at once.

ISBNs and Multiple Distributors (KDP vs IngramSpark)

If you're publishing your book through both Amazon KDP and IngramSpark, you'll need to use two separate ISBNs for your paperback edition — one for each platform. This might sound confusing at first, but it's actually a professional publishing standard.

A. IngramSpark: ISBN #1
   - Used for global bookstore and library distribution (wide reach)
B. Amazon KDP: ISBN #2 (different)
   - Used for direct Amazon printing, faster delivery, and full pricing control

Your readers will never see the difference. Amazon automatically merges both listings under the same product page, showing a single unified book entry. Behind the scenes, however, two ISBNs ensure that each distributor recognizes its own printing edition, avoiding conflicts in metadata, pricing, and royalties.

How to Get One

- **United States:** Buy directly from Bowker (myidentifiers.com).
- **UK:** Nielsen ISBN Agency.
- **Australia:** Thorpe-Bowker Identifier Services.
- **Canada:** Free through Library and Archives Canada.
- **UAE & other regions:** Check your national ISBN agency or use the one for your country of publication.

Cost:

- 1 ISBN: around USD $125 (Bowker)
- 10 ISBNs: around USD $295 (recommended if you plan multiple formats)

Tip: If you use Amazon KDP, they offer a **free ISBN**, but it lists *Amazon* as the publisher.

If you want your publishing imprint (for example, "Amazon Warrior Publishing"), buy your own ISBN.

Owning your ISBN means owning your identity as a publisher.

STEP 2: DESIGNING YOUR BOOK (INSIDE & OUT)

Your book's design determines how it *feels* to the reader — it's your message made tangible.

Don't underestimate the emotional power of beautiful design.

1. The Cover Design

Your cover is your first impression. It must be **clear, professional, and emotionally aligned** with your message.

Front Cover Includes:

- Title and subtitle (crisp, legible fonts).
- Your name (as you want it to appear on Amazon and in libraries).
- Compelling imagery or typography that evokes your book's essence.

Back Cover Includes:

- A short, emotionally resonant blurb (100–150 words).
- A professional author bio (50–70 words).
- ISBN and barcode (bottom right).

Spine:

- Book title, author name, publisher imprint logo (optional).

Pro Tip: Avoid Canva templates for print covers — they're often not sized for printer specs.

Use your cover designer or professional tools (Adobe InDesign, Affinity Publisher) to meet print size requirements.

If you're self-designing:

- Use **KDP's Cover Calculator** (kdp.amazon.com/cover-calculator) to find exact dimensions.
- Check that all text and images are within the "safe zone" (usually 0.125-inch margins).

2. Interior Design (Formatting)

Interior layout impacts readability and professionalism.

Print Formatting Guidelines (Paperback):

- Trim size: 6x9 inches (standard) or 5.5x8.5 for smaller, intimate reads.

- Margins: at least 0.75 inches on all sides.
- Font: Serif fonts like *Garamond, Minion Pro,* or *Georgia* (11–12 pt).
- Line spacing: 1.15–1.5 for comfort.
- Paragraph spacing: Indent first line 0.3–0.5 inches.
- Page numbers centered or outer corners.

eBook Formatting Guidelines:

- Use a clean Word or Google Docs file (no text boxes, no headers/footers).
- Use H1 for chapter titles, H2 for subtitles.
- Export as .docx or .epub.
- Insert page breaks at the end of each chapter.
- Avoid excessive formatting (bolds, italics, colors) — eReaders interpret these differently.

Pro Tip: Run your file through **Kindle Previewer** to check how it appears on phones, tablets, and Kindle devices.

STEP 3: PUBLISHING PLATFORMS — STEP-BY-STEP

You don't need to hire a publishing company. You are one.

Here's how to use the top two self-publishing platforms — **Amazon KDP** and **IngramSpark** — with ease and confidence.

A. Publishing on Amazon KDP (Kindle Direct Publishing)

Amazon KDP is the simplest and most powerful platform for independent authors. It distributes your eBook and paperback to 13+ Amazon marketplaces worldwide.

1. Create an Account:

Go to kdp.amazon.com and sign in with your Amazon account.

2. Set Up Your Book Project:

- Click "+ Create" → "Paperback" or "eBook."
- Enter your title, subtitle, series name (if any), and author name.
- Write your book description (this becomes your Amazon sales page text).
- Add up to 7 keywords and 2 categories (e.g., *Health > Women's Wellness, Self-Help > Creativity*).

3. Upload Manuscript:

- Format as .docx, .pdf, or .epub.
- Use "Look Inside" preview to confirm layout.

4. Upload Cover File:

- Upload a print-ready PDF or use KDP's cover designer.

5. ISBN:

- Use your own (enter it manually) or choose "Free KDP ISBN."

6. Rights & Pricing:

- Select "I own the rights."
- Choose pricing — recommended between $14.99–$22.99 for a 250–350-page healing book.
- KDP automatically calculates your royalties (usually 60% minus print cost).

7. Review and Publish:

Click "Publish Your Paperback."

Amazon will review your file within 72 hours. Once approved, your book is live worldwide.

B. Publishing on IngramSpark (for Bookstores & Libraries)

IngramSpark is essential if you want your book in physical stores or libraries.

It's used by major publishers and independent bookstores alike.

1. Create an Account:

Visit ingramspark.com.

2. Upload Files:

- Print-ready PDF for interior and cover.
- Separate ISBN (cannot reuse your KDP ISBN).

- Trim size and page count must match your KDP file exactly.

3. Set Global Distribution:

IngramSpark connects to 40,000+ retailers, including:

- Barnes & Noble
- Book Depository
- IndieBound
- Libraries and universities

4. Choose Pricing and Discount:

- Standard wholesale discount: 55% (recommended).
- Option to allow returns (bookstores prefer this).

5. Fees:

Ingram charges a $49 setup fee per title (often waived with promo codes).

Pro Tip:

Publish *both* on KDP and IngramSpark.

- KDP = Amazon reach.
- IngramSpark = bookstores and libraries.

This ensures full visibility and backup distribution.

STEP 4: BUILDING YOUR DREAM BOOK TEAM

Even as a self-publisher, you don't have to do everything yourself.

Think of your team as your sacred circle — the people who help bring your message to its highest potential.

1. Editor

There are three main types:

- **Developmental Editor:** Helps with structure, flow, and clarity.
- **Line Editor:** Refines tone, style, and sentence rhythm.
- **Proofreader:** Fixes grammar, spelling, and punctuation.

For healing books: Choose an editor experienced in trauma-informed or memoir writing. They should hold your story gently, not strip its emotion.

2. Cover Designer

Your cover is your book's energetic doorway. Hire a designer who understands your *niche* — healing, spirituality, or women's wellness — and your *reader's aesthetic expectations*. Ask for:

- 3 initial concepts
- Source files (PSD, AI, or InDesign)
- Print-ready versions for KDP and IngramSpark

Recommended Tools (if DIY):

- Canva Pro (for concept mockups)
- BookBrush or Vellum for professional templates

3. Interior Formatter

Formatting ensures your book looks beautiful on every device. You can hire a formatter through:

- Fiverr or Reedsy (search for "KDP interior designer").
- Vellum (Mac-only software for seamless interior design).
- Atticus (Mac & PC alternative).

Checklist for Formatters:

- Include title pages, acknowledgments, and about-the-author page.
- Add page numbers, headers, and consistent font styling.
- Ensure margins are balanced and justified text alignment is clean.

4. Proofreader

Always have a fresh set of eyes before publishing. Even one typo can make a book feel unpolished. Hire someone *not emotionally attached* to your story for the final pass.

STEP 5: CREATING YOUR PUBLISHING IMPRINT

To make your book look and feel professional, you can register your own **publishing imprint** — a business name under which your book is released (e.g., *Amazon Warrior Publishing*).

This adds credibility and professionalism.

Steps to create your imprint:

1. Choose a name that aligns with your brand.
2. Register it as a business (optional, but recommended).
3. Purchase your own ISBNs using that name as the publisher.
4. Create a simple logo for your imprint's spine or copyright page.

Copyright Page Example:

WRITE IT ANYWAY © 2025 Caroline Bakker

All rights reserved. No part of this book may be reproduced without written permission from the publisher.

Published by Amazon Warrior Publishing

ISBN: 978-1-234567-89-0

Printed in the United States of America

STEP 6: EMPOWERMENT THROUGH AWARENESS — LEGAL & ETHICAL ESSENTIALS

Publishing your story is an act of healing *and* an act of ownership. Awareness isn't about fear—it's about empowerment. When you understand the basics that protect your work, you publish from confidence, not confusion.

Copyright = Creative Sovereignty

The moment you write, your words are protected. Registration simply adds proof. Keep dated drafts; that's your evidence of authorship.

Disclaimers Build Trust

If your book touches on wellness or trauma, include one line of integrity:

This book offers education and inspiration, not professional medical or psychological advice.

It tells readers you care about their safety as much as your message.

Respect the Stories You Hold

Change names or get written permission for identifiable people. Your story heals—you don't need to expose others to tell your truth.

Credit What Inspires You

Short quotes are usually fine; full lyrics or long passages need permission. Citing sources honors both ethics and energy.

AI Transparency

If you used AI to organize or polish your book, mention it briefly in your acknowledgments. Honesty models conscious creation.

Business Basics in Plain English

Keep simple records of sales and expenses, and if you plan to publish more than one book, consider a small business or imprint. It's not bureaucracy—it's energetic grounding for the abundance you're calling in.

> **> For more information refer to Appendix A:**
> **Legal & Ethical Essentials for Healing**
> **Authors**

STEP 7: AUTHOR MONEY & PUBLISHING REALITIES

Money conversations don't cheapen art; they stabilize it.

Writing a healing book is emotional work—but publishing it is a business. Understanding costs and royalties helps you make choices from power, not pressure.

Up-Front Investments

Editing ($500–$2 000 avg), cover design ($150–$600), formatting ($100–$400), ISBNs ($125 US / free in Canada), proof copies ($10–$20 each).

Royalties and Pricing

• Amazon KDP ≈ 60% of list price minus print cost.

• IngramSpark ≈ 45–55% after wholesale discount.

Price your book where it feels sustainable *and* accessible (most 250–350 page paperbacks: USD $14.99–$22.99).

Energetics of Earning

Receiving money for your story isn't selling out—it's alignment. Each sale is an energetic exchange: your truth for their transformation.

Long-Tail Income

Your book can evolve into courses, journals, or talks. Think of royalties as roots and your other offerings as branches.

Mindset Mantra

"My story creates impact and income. Both are sacred."

STEP 8: THE FINAL QUALITY CHECKLIST

Before clicking "publish," complete this checklist:

- Title and subtitle consistent everywhere (cover, interior, metadata)
- ISBNs assigned correctly (one per format)
- Table of contents and pagination match
- Front matter and back matter formatted
- Author bio and social links included
- Proof copy ordered and reviewed
- Copyright page accurate

Once you've confirmed everything — hit **publish.** That's the moment your healing story becomes a living, breathing contribution to the world.

STEP 9: CELEBRATE THE MILESTONE

Take time to celebrate this moment — not as an ending, but as a new beginning. You've gone from writer to author, from creator to publisher.

Light a candle. Take yourself out for coffee. Write a note to your future self: *"I did it. I shared my truth with the world."*

Because publishing isn't just logistical — it's *energetic*. You've taken something invisible and made it real. That is alchemy.

Reflection Prompt

What fears arise when you imagine sharing your story publicly?

Write them down — and then write their opposites as affirmations.

Example:

Fear: "What if no one buys my book?"

Affirmation: "The right readers will find my book when they're ready."

WORKSHEET 11 — PUBLISHING LOGISTICS TRACKER

TO BE COMPLETED AFTER READING CHAPTER 15: BECOMING YOUR OWN PUBLISHER

You've written, refined, and aligned your message — now it's time to bring your book into the world.

Becoming your own publisher is an empowering act of ownership. It means you control your creative vision, your income, and the way your story lives in readers' hands.

This worksheet helps you manage the practical steps of publishing *without losing your peace.*

✦ Step 1 — My Publishing Overview

Publishing Element	My Choice / Platform	Notes / Dates / To-Do
ISBN(s)	(List one per format: paperback, hardcover, eBook, audiobook)	
Publishing Platforms	KDP (Amazon), IngramSpark, or both	
Publication Date	(Ideal launch date or soft release window)	
Copyright Registration	Country, year	
Legal Name / Imprint	(Optional: choose a publishing imprint name if desired)	
Book Dimensions	(e.g., 6×9", cream paper)	
Cover Finish	Matte / Gloss / Hardcover	
Interior Type	Black & white / Color	
Retail Price	USD / AED / AUD / EUR	
Keywords & Categories	(For Amazon or Ingram metadata)	

✦ Step 2 — My Book Production Team

Even as an independent author, you don't have to do it alone.

Use this table to track the professionals supporting your project.

Role	Name / Contact	Start Date	Cost / Agreement	Status
Editor				
Proofreader				
Cover Designer				
Interior Formatter				
Illustrator / Photographer (if any)				
Marketing Support				
Virtual Assistant / Admin				

(Tip: Always keep backup copies of contracts, design files, and raw artwork. These are your assets.)

✦ Step 3 — Formatting & Upload Checklist

Amazon KDP (Paperbacks & eBooks)

- ☐ *Format interior as PDF (for print) and EPUB (for eBook)*
- ☐ *Create separate ISBNs for each format*
- ☐ *Upload manuscript and cover files*
- ☐ *Preview with "Look Inside" tool*
- ☐ *Order print proof copy*
- ☐ *Approve for distribution*

IngramSpark (Paperbacks, Hardcovers, Global Distribution)

☐ Format PDF according to Ingram's trim size
and bleed requirements
☐ Upload metadata: title, author, description,
BISAC codes
☐ Set discount (35–55%) and return status
(optional)
☐ Pay upload fee (waived during promotions)
☐ Review and approve print proof

Other Platforms (Optional)

☐ Draft2Digital for eBook aggregation (Apple
Books, Kobo, B&N)
☐ Findaway Voices for audiobooks
☐ Your website shop (direct-to-reader sales)
(Tip: Save all final versions with clear file
names — e.g., "HealingJour-
ney_PRINT_FINAL_v3.pdf.")

✦ Step 4 — Proof Review Notes

When your print proof arrives, take time to review it carefully —
not just for errors, but for energy.

Element	Notes / Revisions Needed
Cover (colors, text placement, feel)	
Interior (margins, fonts, alignment)	
Paper Quality (white vs. cream)	
Spine Text / Title Visibility	
Overall Feeling When Holding It	

"Does this version of my book feel like *me*?"

If yes, approve it.

If not, adjust — this is your masterpiece in physical form.

✦ Step 5 — Publishing Timeline Planner

Use this to plan your milestones with clarity and calm.

Milestone	Target Date	Completed
Final Edit Complete		
Proof Approved		
ISBN Registered		
Upload to KDP		
Upload to IngramSpark		
Order Proof Copy		
Launch / Announcement		
Author Copies Ordered		
Book Live on Amazon		

(Write your dates in pencil — flexibility is part of the process.)

✦ Step 6 — Reflection Prompt

"How does it feel to hold full ownership of my book's creation?

What qualities do I want to embody as a publisher — precision, patience, pride, peace?"

_____

_____

_____

_____

✦ Closing Intention

"I am the creator, the author, and the publisher of my story.

I take responsibility for its form, its beauty, and its journey into the world."

Signature: _____

Date: _____

CHAPTER 16
PRINTING YOUR PROOF
THE FINAL STEP BEFORE THE WORLD SEES YOUR BOOK

W hen I finished writing my first book, I thought it was ready to go. The digital file looked pretty good — every page neat, every heading aligned. Then I printed it.

At first, I had a few early copies made through a small local printer here in Sharjah (United Arab Emirates) — nothing formal, just a quick run to see how it looked and felt in my hands. And that moment changed everything.

The text looked smaller in print than it had on screen. The margins felt tight. The cream paper I chose softened the tone beautifully, but the cover colors printed darker than expected. I began noticing things I had missed a hundred times digitally — small spacing issues, headers slightly off, and sections that felt visually heavy.

So I made changes. I printed it again. And again. Each version revealed something new. Every proof helped me refine both the technical and energetic details of the book — until it finally felt right. That's why this stage matters so much. You can't truly *finish* your book until you've *held* it.

WHY THE PROOF COPY MATTERS

Printing a proof copy is one of the most overlooked yet transformative parts of the self-publishing process. It's where your story moves from idea to embodiment — where you stop editing in theory and start editing through feel.

When you hold your proof, you're not just checking fonts and margins. You're experiencing your book as your reader will. You'll notice pacing, visual rhythm, and even emotional flow differently when it's on paper.

1. START WITH A LOCAL PRINT RUN

Before uploading to any global platform, I recommend printing your first proof locally. Most print shops can produce a short run from a PDF export. This allows you to review paper stock, font size, and overall readability quickly — without waiting for shipping.

My first proofs came from a small printer that bound my file on cream paper. I didn't worry about perfection; I just needed to *see* it. That first experience taught me that publishing is not only creative — it's physical. You learn through touch, weight, and presence.

2. ORDER A PROOF FROM EACH PLATFORM YOU PLAN TO USE

Once your book is formatted and uploaded, order official proofs or author copies from both **Amazon KDP** and **IngramSpark**.

This is one of the best things I did — and one of the most eye-opening.

Amazon KDP Author Copies

KDP proofs tend to ship faster, and their pricing is lower, which is convenient if you're just testing the layout. However, the print quality can vary slightly from batch to batch depending on the printing facility and region. In my experience, the colors printed slightly darker, and the paper quality felt thinner compared to IngramSpark's version.

That said, KDP is perfect for affordability and accessibility. If you're hosting smaller events, book signings, or giveaways, KDP author copies are a practical and budget-friendly choice.

IngramSpark Author Copies

IngramSpark prints felt more polished — the paper thicker, the color tones more consistent, and the overall presentation slightly more professional. IngramSpark also offers global distribution to bookstores and libraries, which means the same file you approve as a proof is what retailers will receive.

When I first received both versions side by side, the difference surprised me. KDP's matte cover had a different texture, slightly lighter in tone. IngramSpark's version had deeper saturation, a crisper spine alignment, and smoother trimming. Neither was "bad," but the energy was distinct.

For example, I found that my *Healing on Empty* proofs from IngramSpark looked more luxurious — something I'd proudly display in bookstores — whereas my KDP author copies felt lighter and easier to ship for direct sales.

The key is not to assume they'll look identical. Always compare them in person before finalizing your settings.

3. REVIEW LAYOUT, TYPOGRAPHY, AND SPACING

Read both proofs cover to cover. Check that:

- Font size and style are consistent.
- Chapter titles are uniform and start on right-hand pages.
- There are no widows or orphans.
- The interior design feels balanced and uncluttered.

If you're using **Vellum**, experiment with slightly adjusting your trim size or margin settings before exporting again. You may need one layout version optimized for print-on-demand (KDP and IngramSpark) and another for local offset printing.

4. MARGINS, GUTTER, AND PAPER FEEL

When comparing proofs, pay attention to small tactile differences:

- The **gutter** (inner margin) on IngramSpark's binding often feels tighter than KDP's, so leave a little extra space when exporting.
- The **paper finish** varies — KDP's cream is slightly yellower, while IngramSpark's cream leans more ivory.
- Page thickness can affect how the book opens and feels.

I didn't realize how much these micro details mattered until I compared them side by side.

5. BLANK PAGES AND SIGNING SPACE

After seeing my first proof, I realized I hadn't left any space for signing or personal dedications.

In the next version, I added two blank pages after the title page — and it made a huge difference during events and readings.

If you plan to sign or personalize copies, always reserve blank pages intentionally.

6. COPYRIGHT, ISBN, AND EDITION DETAILS

Before final approval, verify that all publishing data is correct:

- Copyright year and your full name
- Edition statement (for example, *First Edition, 2025*)
- Your publisher name or imprint (if you have one)
- ISBNs for each version of your book

When using **Vellum**, remember:

- One ISBN for **paperback**
- One for **hardcover** (if applicable)
- One for **ebook**

Once your book is live on both KDP and IngramSpark, order author copies from *each platform* again — not just proofs. These are the same versions readers will receive through retailers. Comparing them will help you make final tweaks to paper choice, color, or pricing for future print runs.

7. CONDUCT A FINAL READ-THROUGH

When your proof copies arrive, don't rush through them. Sit with them.

Notice how your words feel now that they're printed in their final form. Are there small tweaks that still call to you? Does the book flow the way you intended?

Every time I printed a new version, I discovered something small — a better line break, a more balanced font size, a clearer subtitle layout. These final refinements often made the difference between *good* and *beautiful*.

8. TRUST HOW IT FEELS IN YOUR HANDS

This might sound strange, but your body knows when your book is ready.

When I held my fourth version — after multiple local prints, KDP proofs, and IngramSpark copies — I felt it instantly. The energy had shifted. It felt complete.

Publishing isn't just about files and formatting; it's about alignment.

When your book feels balanced — visually, energetically, and emotionally — that's the version the world is meant to hold.

FINAL REFLECTION

Printing your proof is more than quality control. It's an act of embodiment. Each print brings your story one step closer to its truest form. The process might feel repetitive or slow, but every iteration refines your voice and your craft.

When your final author copies arrive — from wherever you choose to print — take a moment to pause.

Feel the paper, smell the ink, trace your name on the cover. This is the moment your invisible work becomes visible. The moment your inner world takes physical form. And the moment you finally see — this isn't just a book.

It's a legacy.

WORKSHEET 12 - AUTHOR COPIES & PROOF COMPARISON GUIDE

Use this checklist to evaluate and compare proof or author copies from **Amazon KDP**, **IngramSpark**, and your **local printer**. Each platform produces slightly different results in print tone, feel, and quality. This guide will help you decide which combination best reflects your book's vision and purpose.

1. Initial Proofs

- Print one early version locally to assess paper feel, size, and layout balance.
- Hold it, flip through it, and make notes on what feels "off" — margins, font size, line spacing, or paper tone.
- Adjust and reprint until it feels visually calm and aligned.

2. Amazon KDP Proofs & Author Copies

- Order a **proof copy** first to confirm formatting, spine width, and color alignment.
- After publication, order **author copies** directly to see the final retail version your readers will receive.
- Check:
  - Paper thickness (KDP cream is slightly yellower and lighter-weight).
  - Cover finish (matte vs. glossy) — color saturation often prints slightly darker.

- Binding alignment and spine centering.

KDP offers fast, affordable printing — ideal for bulk signings, direct sales, or personal stock.

3. IngramSpark Proofs & Author Copies

- Order a **proof** after upload to assess professional bookstore quality.
- After release, order a few **author copies** to compare print consistency.
- Check:
  - Paper color (cream tone is more neutral, slightly ivory).
  - Cover color accuracy — IngramSpark tends to produce truer, richer hues.
  - Spine trimming and overall finish (usually tighter and more precise).

Note: IngramSpark offers global distribution and more consistent bookstore-grade quality.

4. Side-by-Side Comparison

- Place your KDP, IngramSpark, and local proofs next to each other.
- Compare:
  - Weight and thickness
  - Paper color and opacity (how much text shows through)
  - Cover texture and color fidelity
  - Margin depth and text legibility near the spine

- Printing of fine details (logos, illustrations, small fonts)
- Highlight which version best represents your brand tone — luxurious, accessible, minimalist, or natural.

5. ISBNs and Edition Details

- Confirm that each version (ebook, paperback, hardcover) has its own ISBN.
- Double-check edition information (e.g., *First Edition, 2025*).
- Review your copyright and contact details one final time before approving print distribution.

6. The Intuition Test

- Hold each version in your hands.
- Ask yourself: *Which one feels most aligned with my message and my reader?*
- Trust that feeling. It's your compass for quality and authenticity.

Remember:

Every proof brings you closer to alignment. Print, adjust, compare, and refine until your book feels complete — not just in layout, but in energy.

When you can hold it and feel at peace, you'll know:

This is the one I'm proud to share with the world.

CHAPTER 17

FORMAT OPTIONS: EBOOK, PRINT, AND AUDIO

HOW TO DECIDE WHICH FORMATS FIT YOUR MESSAGE AND AUDIENCE

Self-publishing allows your message to travel in many forms—words on a screen, a book in someone's hands, or your voice reaching a listener's heart.

When I first released *The Healing Journey*, I focused only on print because that was familiar. Later I realized that readers experience healing differently: some need to hold a tangible book during their morning ritual, others absorb wisdom through earbuds on a walk.

This chapter explains, in detail, how to create and distribute your book in **eBook**, **print**, and **audio** formats so you can reach every reader without consulting any additional guide.

Before we dive into the practical steps, here's an overview of the most common publishing formats — how they differ, what each one offers, and which might best fit your message and audience

Publishing Formats at a Glance						
Format	Reader Experience	Best For	Production Time	Cost	Royalties	Essence
eBook	Instant digital access worldwide	Fast launches, global reach	Short	Low	~70%	Accessible, flexible
Print Book	Tangible and enduring connection	Credibility, gifts, events	Moderate	Medium	~60%	Grounded, lasting
Audiobook	Immersive, emotional, personal	Auditory learners, intimacy	Moderate–Long	Medium–High	~25–40%	Soulful, embodied
Journal / Workbook	Interactive and reflective	Coaching, courses, self-work	Moderate	Low–Medium	~60–70%	Practical, integrative
Bundle / Course Add-On	Multi-format, scalable learning	Expansion, education, community	Long	High	Variable	Expansive, legacy-building

Each format serves a different kind of reader — and a different part of your message.

Some stories want to be held. Others want to be heard.

The beauty of self-publishing is that you don't have to choose just one. You can start small, release in one format, and expand as your audience grows and your message evolves.

What matters most is intention: meeting your reader where they are, in the way they most naturally receive wisdom.

Let's begin with the simplest, most accessible way to share your story — the eBook.

1. EBOOKS — DIGITAL HEALING AT YOUR READER'S FINGERTIPS

eBooks are the simplest entry point for self-publishers. They cost little to produce and offer global reach.

Benefits

- **Instant access:** readers can download immediately.
- **Low cost:** no printing or shipping.
- **Global reach:** available to international audiences.
- **Easy updates:** you can upload revised editions anytime.

When I published *The Healing Journey*, the eBook allowed women from Canada to Singapore to message me within hours of launch—something print alone could never do.

Technical Specifications

- **File format:** .epub (universal) or .mobi (Kindle legacy).
- **Manuscript setup:** use *Heading 1* for chapters, *Heading 2* for subheadings, insert page breaks after each chapter, and avoid tables or multiple fonts.
- **Export options:** .docx or .epub.
- **Optional formatting tools:** Vellum (Mac), Atticus (PC/Mac), or Reedsy Book Editor (free, browser-based).

Images: minimum 300 dpi, centered, and scaled for mobile screens.

Distribution Platforms

- **Amazon KDP:** largest global reach for Kindle users.
- **Draft2Digital:** aggregates Apple Books, Kobo, and Barnes & Noble.
- **Google Play Books:** strong among Android users.

Recommended price range: USD $4.99–$9.99 (qualifies for Amazon's 70 percent royalty bracket).

2. PRINT BOOKS — TANGIBLE CONNECTION AND CREDIBILITY

A printed book creates physical intimacy between author and reader.

When I held the first proof copy of *The Healing Journey*, I realized that print transforms abstract healing into something tangible and lasting.

Why Print Still Matters

- Readers can annotate and gift physical copies.
- Printed books carry emotional weight and professional credibility.

CHOOSING FORMAT

Choosing Format			
Format	Ideal Use	Advantages	Limitations
Paperback	General readership	Low cost, quick production	Less durable
Hardcover	Premium or library editions	Longevity, perceived value	Higher cost

Begin with paperback; release a hardcover later as a collector's or gift edition.

Print-on-Demand (POD) Platforms

- **Amazon KDP:** free setup, automatic listing on all Amazon marketplaces.

- **IngramSpark:** global bookstore and library distribution (over 40,000 retailers).

Publish on **both**—KDP for Amazon visibility, IngramSpark for bookstores.

Trim Sizes and Paper Choices

- **Trim sizes:** 6×9 in. (standard) or 5.5×8.5 in. (intimate).
- **Paper:** white (for crisp text) or cream (for warmth).
- **Cover finish:** matte for a soft, elegant aesthetic.

Always order a proof copy before launch; visual inspection remains the most reliable quality control (Tschichold 1948).[1]

3. AUDIOBOOKS — THE VOICE OF HEALING

If eBooks provide convenience and print offers connection, audio delivers intimacy. Listening to an author's voice activates empathic resonance in the listener's brain (Schroeder and Lingnau 2021).

Why Audiobooks Matter

- Fastest-growing segment in publishing.
- Ideal for auditory learners and neurodivergent audiences.
- Builds a deeper emotional bond through voice.

CREATING AN AUDIOBOOK ON A BUDGET

Option 1: Record It Yourself

Required equipment

- Quiet, padded room or closet.
- USB microphone (Blue Yeti or Audio-Technica ATR2100x).
- Pop filter and headphones.
- Editing software: *Audacity* (free), *GarageBand* (Mac), or *Adobe Audition* (paid)

Recording guidelines

- Record in 5–10-minute segments per file
- Maintain a 15–20 cm distance from the microphone
- Save each chapter as a separate MP3 file at 192 kbps or higher
- Record intro ("Opening Credits"), outro ("Closing Credits"), and a short retail sample (1–5 minutes)

Audible (ACX) audio specifications

- RMS between −18 dB and −23 dB
- Peaks below −3 dB
- Noise floor below −60 dB
- Consistent volume and pacing across all chapters
- Each file must start with "Chapter [Number or Title]"
- Include both opening and closing credits

Tip: Use *ACX's free "Audio Lab"* tool to check if your files meet technical standards before uploading

Option 2: Hire a Narrator

- **Platforms:** ACX Marketplace, Findaway Voices, Voices.com.
- **Cost:** USD $100–$250 per finished hour; a 60,000-word book ≈ 6 hours.
- A co-narration model—author for reflections, narrator for exposition—can preserve authenticity.

Option 3: Use Production Services

If editing and mastering feel daunting, contract a professional production house. Choose **non-exclusive** distribution so you retain global rights.

Some popular options:

- **Authors Republic** (https://www.authorsrepublic.com) → Upload your finished audio files, or hire their production team. Distributes globally to *Audible, Apple Books, Spotify, Google Play, Kobo, and more.*

- **Findaway Voices by Spotify** (https://findawayvoices.com) → User-friendly platform, supports both exclusive and non-exclusive distribution. You keep full control of your rights and pricing. They now accept AI generated audio books using Elevenlabs. Using this platform you can self publish and distribute your audio book to platform like Audible, Apple Books, Audiobooks.com and many more popular platforms.

- **BookBaby Audio** (https://www.bookbaby.com/audiobooks) → Offers done-for-you services with editing, mastering, and distribution packages.

Does It Matter Which Country You're From?

Yes — **distribution access differs by region:**

- **ACX (Audible's platform)** currently accepts authors **only** from the U.S., U.K., Canada, and Ireland.

However, authors outside those countries can still publish on Audible by:

- Using **Findaway Voices** or **Authors Republic**, which distribute to Audible on your behalf.
- You'll still earn royalties, but your book will be *non-exclusive* (typically 25–40%).
- **Authors in the UAE, Europe, Australia, and other regions** → **Findaway Voices** and **Authors Republic** are your best options. Both allow PayPal or bank transfer payments globally.

Final Tips for Authors

- **Use your author name and brand voice consistently** in your spoken intro and outro.
- **Add a bonus meditation, reflection, or exercise** at

the end of the audiobook — listeners love added value.

- **Retain non-exclusive rights** unless you plan to publish solely on Audible.
- **Submit your audiobook simultaneously with your print and eBook** for maximum visibility during launch week.

4. THE LONG-TERM VALUE OF OWNING YOUR CREATIVE ASSETS

Each file you create—text, audio, or design—is an **intellectual-property asset**.

Owning these assets secures creative and financial independence (Bently and Sherman 2014).

Your Core Assets

- eBook file (.epub)
- Print-ready PDF (interior + cover)
- Audio masters (MP3 or WAV)
- ISBN registrations
- Design and illustration files

With full ownership you can:

- Re-upload or revise anytime.
- Bundle formats into courses or journals.
- Translate or license foreign editions.

When I later expanded *The Healing Journey* into guided meditations for *Meditations by Amazon Warrior*, I used excerpts from my own text—no permissions required.

5. PRICING STRATEGY BY FORMAT

Pricing Strategy by Format

Format	Typical Price (USD)	Royalty Rate	Primary Platform
eBook	4.99 – 9.99	70 % (KDP)	KDP, Draft2Digital
Paperback	14.99 – 22.99	60 % minus print cost	KDP, IngramSpark
Hardcover	24.99 – 29.99	45–55 %	IngramSpark
Audiobook	9.99 – 19.99	25–40 %	ACX, Findaway Voices

Mid-range pricing conveys accessibility while honoring value. Underpricing signals inexperience and diminishes perceived worth (Coker 2022).

WORKSHEET 13 — MULTI-FORMAT PLANNING SHEET

TO BE COMPLETED AFTER READING CHAPTER 17: FORMAT OPTIONS — EBOOK, PRINT, AND AUDIO

Your book isn't limited to one form — it's a living message that can meet readers wherever they are.

Some will hold it in their hands, underline sentences, and keep it by their bed.

Others will listen to your voice on a walk, or read your words quietly on a screen.

This worksheet will help you plan which formats best serve your message, your reader, and your energy.

✦ Step 1 — Format Overview

Format Type	Platform / Distributor	File Type	Production Cost (Est.)	Income Potential	My Reader's Experience	My Decision
eBook	Amazon KDP, Draft2Digital, Apple Books, Kobo	EPUB / MOBI	$0–$100	70% (KDP), varies	Instant global access, searchable, portable	[ ] Include
Paperback	Amazon KDP, IngramSpark	PDF (print interior)	$3–$5 per copy	60% minus print cost	Tangible, giftable, personal connection	[ ] Include
Hardcover	IngramSpark	PDF	$6–$8 per copy	45–55%	Premium edition, ideal for gifts or libraries	[ ] Include
Audiobook	ACX (Audible), Findaway Voices	MP3 / WAV	$0–$1500	25–40%	Deep intimacy through voice, accessibility for busy readers	[ ] Include

(Check or highlight the formats you plan to publish.)

✦ Step 2 — Platform Details & Upload Tasks

Platform	Account Setup Complete (✓)	Upload Needed	Pricing	Launch Date
Amazon KDP				
IngramSpark				
ACX / Findaway Voices				
Draft2Digital				
Author Website (Direct Sales)				

(Tip: Keep all login details and ISBNs recorded in your Publishing Logistics Tracker — Worksheet 11.)

✦ Step 3 — Format Preparation Notes

Use this space to outline the technical and creative needs of each format.

Format	Technical To-Dos	Creative Notes / Opportunities
eBook	Reformat chapters for smaller screens, hyperlink table of contents, test in Kindle Previewer	Add bonus material or links to free resources
Paperback	Ensure proper margins, bleed, and trim size	Include author photo and closing reflection
Hardcover	Adjust spine width, request dust jacket design	Create a collector's edition feel
Audiobook	Record narration, hire engineer, upload sample	Add meditative introduction or bonus track

✦ Step 4 — Financial & Time Planning

Format	Estimated Production Cost	Time Needed	Support / Tools Needed
eBook			
Paperback			
Hardcover			
Audiobook			

(Tip: Always add a 10–15% buffer for unforeseen costs or revisions.)

✦ Step 5 — Reflection Prompts

"Which format best mirrors the *energy* of my book?"

(Example: tactile comfort → paperback, personal presence → audiobook.)

_____

_____

_____

"How does my reader want to experience my story — by holding it, listening to it, or reading on the go?"

_____

_____

_____

"What formats feel aligned with my current resources, and which might I expand into later?"

_____

_____

_____

✦ Step 6 — Long-Term Asset Ownership

Keep a record of your final master files in one secure folder or drive.

Suggested file structure:

/MyBook_Assets

/eBook

/Print

/Audio

/CoverDesign

/Marketing

Add this affirmation to your notes:

"Every file I create is a piece of intellectual property that I own.

I am the guardian of my creative legacy."

CHAPTER 18
MARKETING WITHOUT BURNING OUT

AUTHENTIC VISIBILITY FOR EMPATHS, INTROVERTS, AND HEALERS

Marketing doesn't have to feel like manipulation or self-promotion. It can be a continuation of your message — an invitation for connection.

For many healers, empaths, and introverts, "marketing" sounds like performance. But when you redefine it as *storytelling with purpose*, it becomes something else entirely: a bridge between your heart and your reader's.

When I published *The Healing Journey*, I didn't have a full marketing team or a six-figure launch budget (and I still don't). I had a story, a camera, a website I had built sixteen years earlier, and a sincere desire to help women heal.

That was enough.

USING YOUR STORY AS YOUR BRAND'S HEART

Your story is the heartbeat of your brand.

When I created @healingjourneybook on Instagram, I didn't post polished ads. I shared pieces of the process: notes from editing days, journal pages, quotes that had helped me survive. Those posts built quiet momentum because they were honest.

At the same time, I shared the book on LinkedIn — the tone there was different, more professional and reflective. I spoke about ADHD, PMDD, and women's health in the workplace. I wasn't "selling"; I was starting conversations.

This is what marketing expert Seth Godin calls the **tribe effect** — people connect with you because they see themselves in you (Godin 2008).

People don't buy information; they follow resonance.

The Soul-Aligned Marketing Framework

1. **Clarity:** Who are you serving, and what pain are you helping them heal?
2. **Consistency:** Show up regularly, but sustainably.
3. **Connection:** Lead with conversation, not conversion.

THE GENTLE LAUNCH MODEL: CONNECTION OVER CONVERSION

Traditional book launches often involve countdowns, giveaways, and aggressive posting schedules. That can be effective, but it often burns authors out.

I prefer the **gentle launch model** — a slower, relational approach.

Step 1 Warm-Up Season

Start months before release by sharing your process: quotes, behind-the-scenes photos, your "why."

Readers begin to feel part of the story long before the book exists.

Before I finalised *Write It Anyway,* I started to share a few teaser posts on Instagram and TikTok to create some buzz.

Step 2 Create Visual Trust

Before my first speaking engagement at the **Sharjah Children's Book Festival** — a self-publishing panel hosted by IngramSpark — I hired a professional photographer. Those photos became the foundation of my press kit, my banner, and my digital branding.

I reused that same banner when I spoke at the **House of Wisdom** in Sharjah. The consistency built recognition.

Research on visual memory shows that humans retain imagery

up to 65 percent better than text alone (Paivio 1991). Consistent visuals help your message linger.

If you lack design experience, hire a freelancer on Upwork, Fiverr, or 99designs, or use templates on Canva Pro.

3 Building Your Digital Home

Before Instagram existed, I built carolinebakker.com. It remains my home base — a digital space I control fully. Social media algorithms can shift overnight, but your website is permanent.

Later, I created healingjourneybook.com, a separate site with book resources, journal prompts, and bonus materials. It became a living extension of the book and a search engine anchor for new readers.

You don't need to be a developer to build one. Platforms like Squarespace, Wix, or WordPress make it intuitive.

Author Website Essentials

- Home page: one clear message and call to action.
- About page: your authentic story.
- Books page: covers, blurbs, and buy links.
- Speaking or Media page: photos, bio, downloadable media kit.
- Contact page: professional email or contact form.

Rand Fishkin notes that authentic, long-form content often outperforms paid ads in long-term reach and reader loyalty (Fishkin 2018).

Your website is your anchor; social media is the ripple.

4 Modern Marketing Channels for Authors

Instagram

Great for visual storytelling, quotes, and video reflections.

- Post 2–3 times weekly.
- Mix personal storytelling with short insights from your book.
- Use Stories to show your process, not perfection.

LinkedIn

Perfect for professional storytelling and thought leadership.

- Share lessons learned from your writing or healing process.
- Relate your book's message to workplace well-being or leadership.

YouTube or Podcasts

Ideal for long-form content and connecting through voice.

- Record 5–10 minute videos explaining one key concept per episode.
- Mention your book organically, not as a sales pitch.

Email Newsletter

Still the highest conversion tool in marketing. Start collecting subscribers early by offering something of value, like a chapter sample or affirmation guide.

Industry research shows personal-brand email open rates average between 30–40 percent (Mailchimp 2023).

Amazon Author Central

Create your author profile at author.amazon.com.

Include your bio, social links, upcoming events, and link all your books together. This helps readers discover your body of work.

Goodreads

Claim your author page, connect your book, and thank readers for their reviews. Authentic engagement (not self-promotion) helps visibility.

5 BookTok and the Power of TikTok

BookTok is a subcommunity on TikTok dedicated entirely to books and readers. It has become one of the most influential discovery platforms in publishing.

According to The New York Times, BookTok helped increase U.S. print sales by 43 percent in 2021, primarily in self-published and niche genres (Alter 2022).

For healing authors, BookTok offers something extraordinary: access to organic visibility through authenticity and vulnerability — two things you already embody.

How to Start on BookTok

1. **Create a TikTok account** with your author name or book title.
2. **Post short, real clips** — you do not need to dance or follow trends. Speak from the heart.
3. **Ideas for content:**
    - Reading a short passage aloud.
    - Sharing the story behind your book cover.
    - Talking about one lesson your book taught you.
    - Filming peaceful scenes (forest walks, journaling) with a short voice-over from your text.
4. **Use relevant hashtags:**
    - #BookTok #HealingJourney #ADHDAwareness #WomensHealthBooks #SelfPublishingAuthor
5. **Engage intentionally:** comment on similar creators' posts. BookTok thrives on community.

Consistency over Virality

It's better to post one authentic video a week than ten forced ones. TikTok's algorithm rewards watch time and connection, not perfection.

Marketing expert Donald Miller reminds authors that every post should serve the reader's story, not the writer's ego (Miller 2017).

When you post with service in mind — "What might my reader need to hear today?" — you build emotional loyalty, not fleeting likes.

6 When You Don't Have Time or Technical Skills

Not everyone enjoys digital marketing, and that's okay.

If technology overwhelms you, delegate small pieces rather than the entire strategy.

- Hire a **virtual assistant** for scheduling.
- Work with a **designer** for graphics and banners.
- Outsource **SEO or email setup** once your foundation is built.

If you have limited funds, prioritize:

1. Professional photography (credibility).
2. A clean, simple website.

Simon Sinek's *Start with Why* reminds us that clarity of purpose attracts more loyalty than production value (Sinek 2009).

When your message is clear, every post becomes a ripple of service.

7 Managing Energy and Avoiding Digital Burnout

Marketing works best when your nervous system feels safe. The more grounded you are, the more your message lands.

Energy-Safe Marketing Practices

- Set posting hours and log off after them.

- Batch content weekly to reduce decision fatigue.
- Use automation tools (Later, Planoly, Buffer) for scheduling.
- Take social media rest days.

Occupational psychology research shows that planned digital rest increases creativity and prevents emotional exhaustion (Kinnunen et al. 2019).

8 The Energetics of Visibility

Visibility is not vanity; it is service.

Every post, story, or email becomes an act of offering — not of performance.

When you see marketing as an extension of healing, not an interruption of it, it becomes easier to sustain.

You don't need to go viral. You need to go authentic.

Reflection Prompt

Which marketing platform feels most aligned with your energy right now — Instagram, LinkedIn, TikTok, or your website?

What small action could you take this week to show up there with honesty and ease?

WORKSHEET 14 — GENTLE LAUNCH MAP

TO BE COMPLETED AFTER READING CHAPTER 18: MARKETING WITHOUT BURNING OUT

Launching your book doesn't have to mean overwhelm, endless posting, or pressure to "go viral."

You can release your work in a way that feels spacious, authentic, and aligned with your energy.

This worksheet will help you design a **Gentle Launch Plan** — one that honors connection over conversion, and meaning over metrics.

✦ Step 1 — Set Your Energetic Intention

Before strategy, comes energy.

What do you want your launch to *feel like*?

Grounded? Playful? Intentional? Expansive?

"When people encounter my book for the first time, I want them to feel…"

_____

_____

Now write your **launch affirmation:**

"I share my story with ease, trust, and authenticity.

The right readers will find it — and feel seen."

✦ Step 2 — The Four Phases of a Gentle Launch

Every launch has its seasons. Instead of rushing everything into one week, spread your energy across these four stages.

Phase	Purpose	What to Focus On	My Actions / Notes
1. Warm-Up (4–8 weeks before launch)	Build anticipation through connection.	Share behind-the-scenes glimpses, reflections, snippets of your writing journey. Reintroduce your story and why it matters.	
2. Pre-Launch (2–3 weeks before release)	Create curiosity and trust.	Announce your release date, post quotes or short video clips, and invite early readers or ARC reviewers.	
3. Launch Week	Celebrate and share.	Post your cover, hold a small virtual event, speak on podcasts, or share a heartfelt story about what this book means to you.	
4. Integration (Post-Launch)	Rest and reconnect.	Share gratitude, repost reader feedback, and take time off social media to ground yourself again.	

(Tip: Think of marketing as storytelling — not selling. Each post, interview, or event is another chance to connect through truth.)

✦ Step 3 — Platform Alignment

Choose the marketing channels that feel most natural to you.

You don't need to be everywhere — you just need to be *present* somewhere.

Platform	Purpose	My Focus / Frequency
Instagram / Bookstagram	Visual storytelling, connection	
TikTok / BookTok	Quick, relatable video storytelling	
LinkedIn	Professional storytelling, thought leadership	
YouTube / Podcast	Long-form voice and teaching	
Email Newsletter	Deep connection and updates	
Author Website	Central hub for all info and purchase links	

(Tip: Choose 2–3 platforms max for your main focus. Consistency matters more than quantity.)

✦ Step 4 — Story-Based Content Ideas

Your content should be an *extension of your message*. Use these prompts to create authentic, heart-led posts or reels:

- The *moment* I knew I had to write this book...
- What I wish someone had told me when I was healing...
- 3 lessons my journey taught me about resilience...
- Why I chose to self-publish (and what I learned along the way)...
- My favorite line from my book (and what it means to me)...

"Marketing is simply storytelling with a purpose — and your story is already powerful enough."

✦ Step 5 — Visibility Boundaries

Marketing doesn't mean constant exposure. Create gentle boundaries to protect your nervous system:

Area	My Boundary / Plan
Screen time limit per day	
When I check messages or analytics	
How often I post	
How I'll ground myself after sharing vulnerable content	
Who I can ask for help (friend, assistant, VA)	

(Example: "I'll post three times a week, check comments once daily, and rest offline on weekends.")

✦ Step 6 — Launch Support Circle

List the people who can help you — emotionally or practically.

This could include your editor, designer, friends, fellow authors, or online community.

Support Role	Name / Contact	How They Can Help
Accountability Partner		
Virtual Assistant		
Photographer / Videographer		
Book Reviewers / Beta Readers		
Family / Friends for Emotional Support		

✦ Step 7 — Reflection Prompts

"What feels most aligned and joyful about sharing my book?"

_____

_____

_____

"What parts of marketing tend to drain me, and how can I approach them differently?"

_____

_____

_____

"What does success mean for *this* launch — beyond sales or numbers?"

_____

_____

_____

✦ Step 8 — Closing Intention

"My launch is an extension of my healing — not a test of my worth.

I choose slow growth, soulful connection, and sustainability over stress."

Signature: _____

Date: _____

CHAPTER 19
BUILDING YOUR AUTHOR BRAND

AUTHOR PLATFORM BASICS THAT WON'T FRY YOUR NERVOUS SYSTEM

HOW TO POSITION YOURSELF AS A THOUGHT LEADER OR GUIDE

Most people think they need to be *someone* before they can lead — verified, famous, perfectly branded. But here's the truth no one tells you: **you don't.**

When I launched my first book *The Healing Journey*, I wasn't a New York Times bestseller or an influencer. I was a mother navigating ADHD and PMDD, rebuilding my nervous system, and running a small coaching practice. I had no publisher. No PR team. Just my voice — and the courage to use it.

And that was enough.

By the time I clicked *Publish* for the first time, I already had a foundation: years of honest writing, an email list I'd built one subscriber at a time, and a small but loyal community that trusted me because I told the truth — not the highlight reel.

That's what an author platform really is. It's not about numbers. It's about **connection**.

WHAT IS AN AUTHOR PLATFORM?

An author platform is the ecosystem of trust, connection, and visibility you build around your message. It's how readers find you, believe you, and grow with you.

It includes:

- Your website or online hub
- Your email list (even if it starts with ten people you know)
- Your social media or content channels
- Your visibility through speaking, podcasting, or collaborations
- Your story, values, and message — shared consistently

Here's what most people forget: **you are the brand.**

Not your book — *you.*

People don't follow books. They follow *humans.* They follow energy, honesty, and resonance. When you share your truth, even in small ways, you become the lighthouse — and your book becomes the beam of light that travels outward.

If you're thinking, *"But I don't have an audience yet,"* start where you are. Think of your current connections — friends, colleagues, the barista who knows your order. Those are real people. Add them to your circle (with permission) and nurture those relationships.

You don't need to be loud. You just need to be consistent.

Your lived experience is your brand.

Your body of work is how it spreads.

1. Becoming the Messenger of Your Message

When *The Healing Journey* came out, I thought my work was done. But soon I realized the book hadn't just created something new — it had *created me.*

It gave me new identities to grow into: Author. Teacher. Messenger.

The book wasn't the final chapter. It was the beginning of a brand rooted in authenticity and healing.

Lesson: You don't need to *look* like a brand. You need to *live* your message.

2. Integrating Your Book Into Your Offerings

Your book is the seed. Everything else — courses, meditations, retreats, talks — are the branches.

After *The Healing Journey*, readers wanted to go deeper. They didn't just want to read; they wanted to *experience* the transformation. That's how my Insight Timer courses were born:

- *Mindfulness for Women with ADHD* — daily tools for emotional regulation.
- *5 Days of Mindfulness* — a gentle, immersive reset.

Both offerings were natural extensions of my book.

Mistake I Made: I tried to launch too many things at once — courses, meditations, YouTube series — and ended up overwhelmed.

What Worked: Focusing on one aligned offering and giving it my full energy.

Instead of asking, *"What can I create next?"* ask:

> *"What transformation from my book do I want*
> *to expand on first?"*

Your readers want to keep walking with you after the final page.

Give them a next step — just one.

3. Speaking: From Page to Stage

My first speaking invitation came from IngramSpark — a panel called *Beyond the Manuscript* at the Sharjah Children's Reading Festival.

I almost said no. I didn't feel ready. But I went anyway.

I didn't speak to impress. I spoke to connect — to the woman silently nodding in the audience, feeling seen for the first time.

That talk led to a press feature (*From Burnout to Bestseller*) and later to my keynote, *She Rises: A Journey to Inner Peace,* at the House of Wisdom.

Lesson: You don't wait until you're ready. You *become* ready by saying yes before you believe you are.

Speaking isn't about selling — it's about serving.

4. Building Your Author Ecosystem

Once your message is clear, it's time to give it a home.

a. Goodreads & Amazon Author Pages

These aren't vanity profiles — they're credibility anchors.

- Claim your books and check details.
- Add a personal bio, photo, and website.
- Post updates or respond to reviews.
- Join Q&As or giveaways.

Check in monthly to keep it fresh. You don't need to be famous — just *real.*

b. Your Website — Your Digital Home

Social media is borrowed land. Your website is *yours.*

Keep it clean, clear, and heartfelt. Include:

1 Homepage: Who you are, what you do, and links to your book or freebie.

2 About Page: Your story and mission (300–800 words).

3 Book Page: Cover, blurb, purchase links, and testimonials.

4 Contact Page: Easy way to reach you.

5 Email Opt-In: Offer a free meditation, PDF, or guide.

Tip: Squarespace for simplicity, WordPress for blogging, or even a Canva/MailerLite landing page if you're just starting.

People will Google your name the moment your book launches — make sure what they find represents you well.

c. Build Your Email List

Your email list is your most valuable asset. No algorithms. No noise. Just connection.

Start with something simple:

- "Download my free sleep meditation."
- "Get my ADHD & PMDD Morning Checklist."
- "Join my behind-the-scenes author updates."

Send monthly updates — reflections, stories, or sneak peeks. The goal isn't to sell. It's to build trust.

5. Your First Book Is the Foundation, Not the Finish Line

Publishing your first book isn't the end — it's the *beginning* of your body of work.

Your book establishes credibility and direction. From there, you can grow into:

- Courses
- Retreats
- Podcasts
- Coaching programs
- Speaking engagements

The Healing Journey became the foundation for everything I do now — meditations, coaching, and wellness products — all rooted in one message: **healing is possible.**

Each future book refines your message. Each talk expands your reach. Each offering deepens your impact.

As Simon Sinek reminds us, *"People don't buy what you do; they buy why you do it."*

Your book is your *why* in tangible form.

Reflection Prompt

If your book were a doorway, what would it open into — a course, a talk, a community?

Write down one actionable next step to expand your message this year.

WORKSHEET 15 — AUTHOR ECOSYSTEM MAP

TO BE COMPLETED AFTER READING CHAPTER 19: BUILD YOUR AUTHOR IDENTITY

Your book is not the end of your journey — it's the foundation of your body of work.

It's the heartbeat that can flow into everything else you create: talks, courses, meditations, podcasts, communities, and more. This worksheet helps you connect the dots — to see how your message can live, breathe, and serve beyond the page.

✦ Step 1 — Map Your Core Message

Every ecosystem begins with one truth — the message at the center of your work.

Write yours clearly here:

"The core message of my book — and my work — is…"

_____

_____

_____

_____

(Examples: "Healing begins with self-awareness." / "Your story can be your medicine." / "Regulation is the path to resilience.")

This message becomes your **north star.** Everything you create will point back to it.

✦ Step 2 — The Author Ecosystem Visual

Draw or visualize your ecosystem as a **circle or tree**. At the center: your book. Around it: the offerings, platforms, and extensions that naturally flow from it. Use this table to brainstorm what your "branches" could look like.

Core Element	Examples / Ideas	My Next Step or Vision
Book(s)	Current title + future series or companion journal	
Courses / Workshops	Online courses, Insight Timer programs, live masterclasses	
Speaking	Keynotes, panels, wellness events, retreats	
Meditations / Audio	Spotify, YouTube, Insight Timer guided sessions	
Coaching / Consulting	1:1 sessions, mentorship for authors, wellness coaching	
Community / Membership	Patreon, private group, book club, or healing circle	
Products / Brand Extensions	Journals, affirmation cards, apparel, holistic products	
Digital Presence	Website, email list, social platforms, podcast	

(Tip: Choose only a few focus areas to start. You can grow gradually — one branch at a time.)

✦ Step 3 — Identify Your Pillars

Your pillars are the repeating themes that appear in your writing, teaching, and speaking. They become your signature — what people know you for.

On the following page, list 3–5 recurring themes from your book that feel timeless and true.

Pillar / Theme	Why It Matters to My Work

(Example: Mindfulness, Nervous System Healing, Feminine Leadership, Authentic Storytelling, Self-Compassion.)

✦ Step 4 — Reader → Student → Community Flow

Your reader's journey doesn't end after reading your book.

This section helps you visualize how they might continue engaging with you.

Stage	Reader's Experience	Your Offering / Next Step
Reader	Finds your book and resonates with your message	Book → free download → website visit
Follower / Subscriber	Connects with your ongoing content or newsletter	Weekly posts, videos, or mini reflections
Student / Client	Wants to go deeper	Online course, mentorship, or retreat
Community Member	Becomes part of your ecosystem	Book club, private group, or membership

"Your book is the doorway — but your ecosystem is the home they enter."

✦ Step 5 — Reflection Prompts

"Which branches of my author ecosystem feel most alive or exciting right now?"

_____

_____

_____

"What parts of my book naturally lend themselves to teaching, speaking, or guided experiences?"

_____

_____

_____

"What does being a thought leader mean to me — in my own words?"

_____

_____

_____

✦ Step 6 — Closing Intention

"My book is the seed, and I am the soil.

I will nurture my message and let it grow into whatever forms it's meant to take."

Signature: _____

Date: _____

CHAPTER 20
STAYING GROUNDED THROUGH VISIBILITY

WHAT HAPPENS EMOTIONALLY AFTER YOU HIT PUBLISH.

POST-LAUNCH EMOTIONS

The launch is over. The book is live. You've posted the announcement, thanked your supporters, maybe even signed your first few copies. And then, **silence**.

This is the moment few authors talk about—the quiet after creation, the strange emptiness that follows the adrenaline of release.

Brené Brown calls it a **"vulnerability hangover"**—the emotional crash that happens after you share something deeply personal with the world (Brown 2012).

You've opened your heart, told your story, and suddenly you realize: people can read it, interpret it, and even judge it.

That awareness can feel raw.

When *The Healing Journey* came out, I expected joy and relief. Instead, I felt exposed. I would wake up in the night wondering: *Did I share too much? Did I say it right? What if someone misunderstands?*

Those thoughts are normal.

They're not signs of weakness; they're signs that you've shared something real.

1. THE EMOTIONAL LANDSCAPE AFTER PUBLISHING

Publishing a healing book is unlike releasing fiction or a business manual—it's an act of self-revelation.

You've shared pieces of your life that once lived in private journals. That requires courage, but it also requires recovery.

Common post-launch feelings include:

- **Emptiness:** After months of focus, you suddenly have space—and the nervous system doesn't know what to do with it.
- **Fear of judgment:** You may worry about how family, colleagues, or readers will perceive your honesty.
- **Pressure to perform:** You might feel you need to "maintain momentum" or chase sales immediately.
- **Imposter syndrome:** That inner voice might whisper, "Who are you to teach this?"

The best antidote is rest and reflection.

Remember: your job was to *birth* the book. The marketing, reviews, and reader responses belong to the book's life, not yours.

Psychologist Mihaly Csikszentmihalyi described the "flow hangover" that often follows peak creative focus—when the brain, having operated in full engagement, needs time to recalibrate (Csikszentmihalyi 1990).

Rest isn't indulgence; it's neurological integration.

2. SETTING ENERGETIC AND DIGITAL BOUNDARIES

Once your book is public, your inbox may fill with messages, invitations, and comments—both kind and critical. It's vital to protect your emotional bandwidth.

Energetic Boundaries

- **Separate the self from the story.** The book is not you; it's an artifact of who you were when you wrote it.
- **Ground daily.** Spend time offline, walk barefoot, or use breathwork before reading reviews or messages.
- **Create rituals of closure.** Light a candle or journal a thank-you letter to your book each night during launch week. This helps your body release attachment.

Digital Boundaries

- Schedule social media check-ins rather than scrolling impulsively.
- Delegate review monitoring to a trusted friend or assistant if needed.
- Resist the urge to refresh sales dashboards. Progress is cumulative, not hourly.

Neuroscience shows that constant metric-checking activates the brain's reward circuits similarly to gambling, increasing anxiety and dopamine depletion (Turel, He, and Xue 2021).

Protect your focus by staying mindful of your digital habits.

When you protect your energy, you protect the sustainability of your purpose.

3. LETTING THE BOOK HAVE ITS OWN LIFE

Once published, your book begins to move through the world on its own terms. It will reach people you've never met, in ways you can't predict.

Some will read every word. Some will only read the back cover and feel seen. Some will never finish it—but that doesn't mean you failed.

When I released *The Healing Journey*, I expected constant engagement. Instead, weeks would go by without hearing from readers. Then suddenly, an email would appear:

"Your story helped me see my ADHD differently."

"I read your chapter on PMDD and cried—it felt like you were describing me."

That's when I learned something profound: the impact of your book often happens quietly, long after you've let go.

Author Elizabeth Gilbert writes that once a creative work is released, it "belongs to everyone who encounters it—and not one bit more to you" (Gilbert 2015).

It becomes a relationship between reader and page, spirit and story.

Your task now is to let it breathe.

You can still nurture your book—by speaking about it, teaching from it, or expanding on its themes—but you must also give it autonomy.

You are no longer the sole custodian of its meaning.

4. RETURNING TO CENTER

After the intensity of launch, your nervous system needs gentleness.

Here's how to stay grounded while your book lives in the world:

1. Rest and Reclaim Space: Take a week—or even a month— away from creation. Sleep, cook, walk, move your body. This recalibration prevents burnout and restores creative clarity (Maslach and Leiter 2016).

2. Reconnect with Joy: Do something unrelated to writing: garden, travel, paint, or play with your children. You've spent months focused outward; this brings you back inward.

3. Reflect on What You Learned: Journal on three questions:

- What did writing and publishing teach me about myself?
- What surprised me about readers' responses?
- What do I feel called to explore next?

4. Begin Listening for the Next Message: When the time is right, you'll feel another whisper—another story asking to be told. It might not be a book; it might be a talk, a course, or a poem. But it will come from the same place: truth seeking expression.

5 Trust the Ripple: Most people who read your book will never message you. But that doesn't mean it didn't move them. Just because you can't see the ripple doesn't mean it's not happening.

Your story might sit on a shelf for months before reaching the right reader on the right day. You may never know the full impact—and that's the beauty of it. Let go of ownership. Let go of outcome. Your role was to write it honestly and release it courageously. Everything beyond that is grace.

Reflection Prompt

How does it feel in your body when you think about people reading your story?

Write about what boundaries—energetic, emotional, or digital—you want to keep in place as your book continues its journey.

WORKSHEET 16 — POST-LAUNCH SELF-CARE PLAN

TO BE COMPLETED AFTER READING CHAPTER 20: STAYING GROUNDED WHEN IT'S OUT IN THE WORLD

You've done something extraordinary: you brought your story into the world.

Now it's time to nurture the storyteller.

This worksheet is your permission slip to rest, reconnect, and rebuild your energy after your book's release.

Because when you care for the author, you protect the legacy of the work.

✦ Step 1 — Emotional Check-In

Take a deep breath, close your eyes, and ask yourself:

"How do I actually feel right now that my book is out?"

Feeling Word	Intensity (1–10)	What I Need Most Right Now
Relief		
Pride		
Fear		
Emptiness		
Gratitude		
Exhaustion		
Joy		
Uncertainty		

(Add or circle the emotions that resonate. There's no "should.")

✦ Step 2 — Re-Center Your Nervous System

Create a list of grounding tools that help you feel steady when your mind spirals into "What next?" or "Was it enough?"

Regulation Tool	When I'll Use It	Notes / Support Needed
Breathwork (4-7-8 or box breathing)		
Nature walk / sun time		
Movement (yoga, swim, dance)		
Journaling or body scan		
Digital detox days		
Massage / energy healing / therapy		
Connection with trusted friend or partner		

Mantra: "I can slow down now. My book knows how to travel without me."

✦ Step 3 — Digital and Energetic Boundaries

Define how you'll interact with the online world post-launch.

Area	Boundary / Plan
Checking sales stats or reviews	
Responding to messages and DMs	
Social media time limits	
Handling criticism or unsolicited feedback	
Time off before the next project	

(Tip: Silence can be sacred. Let yourself step away without apology.)

✦ Step 4 — Replenishment Ritual

Choose 3 activities that fill your cup after months of output.

1

2

3

Examples: a weekend retreat, quiet mornings with no schedule, creative play unrelated to writing, or time with loved ones.

Affirmation: "I give myself permission to rest without guilt. Rest is part of the creative cycle."

✦ Step 5 — Reflection Prompts

"What surprised me most about life *after* publishing?"

_____

_____

"What does success feel like in my body — not on paper?"

_____

_____

"What lessons do I want to carry into my next creative season?"

_____

_____

✦ Step 6 — Support Circle Inventory

List the people and practices that can hold you while you recalibrate.

Name / Resource	How They Support Me	How I Can Ask for Help

✦ Step 7 — Closing Intention

Light a candle, stretch, or place your hands on your heart as you read this aloud:

"I've done my part.

I release my book to its own journey.

I return to stillness, trusting that my words are working in ways I may never see."

Signature: _____

Date: _____

PART SIX
BEYOND THE BOOK
WHEN YOUR STORY BECOMES
SOMETHING BIGGER

CHAPTER 21
WRITING CHANGED ME
HOW WRITING HEALS YOU BEFORE IT HELPS ANYONE ELSE

As you know by now, when I wrote my first book, *The Healing Journey: Navigating Adult ADHD & PMDD*, I had no formal training, no publishing background, and no big-name team behind me.

I had journals, a head full of thoughts, and a heart full of pain I was desperate to make sense of.

I was burning out—juggling ADHD, PMDD, motherhood, and the emotional weight of everything I hadn't yet processed. Writing became my anchor. It gave shape to the chaos and helped me find meaning in the mess.

And I'm so glad I started. I didn't wait until I had it all figured out. I followed the nudge. I wrote messy. I rewrote. I doubted myself. I kept going. I published. And in doing so, I remembered who I was. **It reminded me: I can do hard things.**

YOU'LL GROW FROM THIS—EVEN IF NO ONE ELSE SEES IT

The transformation didn't come from the finished book—it came from the process. Writing didn't just make me more diligent or disciplined; it made me more honest. It gave my soul a true voice.

It helped me sit with discomfort, push through doubt, and keep showing up on days when I felt like hiding. It gave me structure when my life felt anything but structured. It reminded me that my story matters. And once I saw that, I couldn't unsee it.

I began noticing how ordinary moments—walks, meditations, kitchen-sink reflections—turned into stories. The more I wrote, the more those stories revealed their purpose.

WRITING OPENS DOORS YOU DON'T EVEN KNOW EXIST

I never expected much beyond the personal healing. But putting my book out there changed everything.

Not long after I self-published through IngramSpark, I was invited to speak at the **Sharjah Children's Reading Festival** in the UAE on a panel for IngramSpark.

Me—on stage—talking about my healing journey, ADHD and PMDD story, and the power of writing. It was vulnerable. It was raw. It was beautiful. And it had ripple effects I never imagined.

Since then, I've spoken on stages, received messages from readers who felt less alone, and been approached for collaborations and coaching.

The book created credibility—but more than that, it became a **lighthouse**. When you write your truth, you light the way for others to find theirs.

DON'T WAIT TO BE PERFECT—JUST KEEP WRITING

Your first book won't be perfect. It's not meant to be. Your second one might not be either.

But every book will make you better.

It's not about the outcome—it's about the journey: sitting with your thoughts, learning something new, making mistakes, trying again, and refusing to give up on yourself. That's the real gold.

I edited my first book multiple times after publishing (and I did the same with this book). Changed the subtitle. Fixed typos. Updated the formatting. Re-uploaded it more times than I can count. That didn't make me a failure—it made me a finisher.

Here's what I learned:

- Don't wait for perfection—it's a moving target.
- You can always revise later or release a second edition.
- The sooner your book is out, the sooner it starts helping people.
- Once it's out, you'll have space to move forward.

Most people treat their book like the final destination. But really —it's the beginning.

CHAPTER 22
AFTER YOU HIT PUBLISH
THE LONG GAME OF AUTHORSHIP AND EXPANSION

M ost authors hit "publish" and expect the journey to end. But here's the truth:

that's when it truly begins.

Your book is no longer just yours—it's out in the world, breathing, traveling, and making an impact beyond you. Some days, you'll feel the rush of accomplishment. Other days, an anticlimactic crash—"Is that it?"

This chapter is your roadmap for what happens next: how to stay grounded, keep momentum, and let your book expand far beyond its pages.

LET YOUR BOOK WORK FOR YOU

Publishing is like planting a seed. What you do next determines how far those roots grow.

1. Use Your Book to Book Speaking Gigs

You're not just a writer—you're now an author with a message. Conferences, wellness events, schools, libraries, and podcasts are always seeking authentic stories.

Prepare:

- A short speaker pitch featuring your book.
- A professional photo and concise bio.
- 2–3 topics you can speak on that connect to your book's message.

Books open doors that social media can't. When you hold up a published book, people listen differently—it signals authority and authenticity.

2. Turn Your Book Into a Course or Coaching Program

If your book includes steps, tools, or transformation frameworks—this is gold. Your chapters can become modules; your stories can anchor lessons.

Ways to expand:

- A video course, audio series, or live workshop.
- Printable worksheets, meditations, or checklists.
- Group coaching or 1:1 guidance for readers who want to go deeper.

3. Let It Be Your Credibility Bridge

Your book is your calling card. Send it to potential partners, media contacts, or organizations you dream of working with. Let it open conversations that once felt out of reach.

HANDLE REVIEWS LIKE A PROFESSIONAL

Reviews will come—some glowing, some critical. How you respond matters.

Celebrate the Good Ones:

- Thank reviewers personally (with permission).
- Share excerpts in newsletters or social posts.
- Keep a "Kind Words" folder for the hard days.

Respond Gracefully to Criticism:

Not every review will be kind—or fair. When it happens, breathe.

You can simply say:

"Thank you for your honest feedback. Every perspective helps me grow as a writer and human."

Privately, ask yourself:

- Is there something useful to learn?
- Or is this more about their lens than my truth?

A book that offends no one rarely impacts anyone.

EMBRACE THE LIVING BOOK MODEL

Books aren't fixed; they evolve with you.

Release Revised Editions — add a foreword, expand a chapter, or update research.

A second edition isn't failure; it's proof you've grown.

Create Companion Materials — journals, workbooks, or meditations that help readers integrate your message.

Expand into Other Mediums — audiobooks, podcasts, live events, retreats. Each one extends your reach without reinventing the wheel.

WHAT NOW? RIDING THE WAVE WITHOUT DROWNING

The post-launch gap is real. I wish someone had warned me.

After all the energy it took to write, edit, format, and finally hit *Publish*, I expected fireworks. Instead, I felt quiet—almost empty. I call it the *book-baby blues*.

At first, I didn't even plan a big launch. I just wanted to hold the book in my hands. So I uploaded to Amazon KDP, ordered a proof, and waited.

The first version wasn't perfect—spacing errors, awkward breaks. So I uploaded Version 2. Then 3. Then 4. By Version 5, I finally let it be. I realized that if I kept waiting for perfect, I'd never publish anything. *Done is better than perfect.*

Then came the vulnerability hangover. My private story was public. Anyone could judge it. I refreshed Amazon far too often, searching for validation.

What steadied me was remembering *why* I wrote the book. I

didn't publish to be perfect—I published because the story was done living inside me.

That shift changed everything. Once I remembered my why, numbers stopped defining me. Praise didn't inflate me, and silence didn't deflate me. The book had already done its job: it existed.

Here's your anchor:

- Rest, but don't disappear—stay connected in small, genuine ways.
- Reflect on your process—what felt aligned? what drained you?
- Jot new ideas without pressure; they'll come.
- Stay in touch with readers. One heartfelt message— "Thank you, I thought I was the only one"—can remind you it was all worth it.

And when the time feels right, you'll write again. Not because you have to, but because you'll feel the tug.

TRUST THE RIPPLE EFFECT

Here's the part you may never see: many readers will never leave a review or send an email. But they're out there—and your words mattered.

Your book may have helped someone through a dark night, reminded them to keep going, or shown them they weren't alone. That's the sacred ripple effect of publishing: your courage plants seeds that may bloom years later, in lives you'll never meet.

CHAPTER 23
YOUR STORY IS THE MEDICINE
THE RIPPLE BEYOND YOU

There will come a moment—after the writing, editing, publishing, and promoting—when you'll realize something quietly profound.

This was never just about a book.

It was about becoming who you needed to be to write it.

You didn't just create pages—you created transformation.

Every sentence was a reclamation of your voice.

Every chapter a doorway back to your truth.

That's the real work of writing a healing book—it heals you first.

But it doesn't stop there.

Once your story leaves your hands, it ripples outward.

Someone will read your words at 2 a.m., tears falling, realizing they're not alone.

Someone else will underline a line that lands like medicine.

Another will close the book and whisper, *"Maybe I can heal too."*

That's the ripple. And it keeps moving—through hearts, homes, and generations.

YOUR STORY IS THE MEDICINE

In writing your truth, you've done something radical in a world that rewards silence and surface.

You've turned pain into purpose. You've proven that honesty itself can heal.

Your book is living proof that vulnerability is strength.

Its power doesn't depend on bestseller lists or algorithms; it lives in the lives it touches.

"Telling our stories creates community, builds bridges, and can save lives."

— Anne Lamott, *Almost Everything: Notes on Hope* (2017)

THE RIPPLE OF COURAGE

Every creative act sends a message to the collective: *I'm not afraid to be seen anymore.*

When one person stands in truth, others find courage to do the same.

Think of your story as a small stone dropped into still water—

you may not see the edges it reaches, but the waves keep expanding long after the splash.

YOU ARE THE CONTINUATION

You've learned to write with honesty, edit with compassion, publish with sovereignty, and share with integrity.

Now you're ready for the next chapter—not of the book, but of your becoming.

Maybe that means another manuscript.

Maybe a course, a talk, a movement.

Maybe simply living your life with more gentleness and courage.

Whatever form it takes, it's part of the same creative current that guided you here.

Trust it. Follow it. Write it anyway.

Reflection Prompt: Write a short letter to your future self, one year from now.

Thank yourself for the courage it took to write and share your truth.

Describe how you want your story to keep rippling outward—through your words, your work, and your presence.

CHAPTER 24

THE 30-DAY SELF-PUBLISHING ROADMAP

YOUR GENTLE GUIDE TO FINISH, PUBLISH & SHARE YOUR HEALING STORY

You've made it to the end of *Write It Anyway.* You've walked through fear, healing, awakening, and truth-telling.

But this isn't the end—it's the beginning of your next chapter.

Whether you're staring at a blank page or polishing your draft, these next four weeks are your invitation to stay connected to your voice, your story, and your purpose—especially when life gets loud.

This is your integration period—a structured yet gentle roadmap to help you build momentum, self-trust, and courage as you turn your story into a finished book that helps others heal too.

WEEK 1 — FOUNDATION & FINAL DRAFT (DAYS 1–7)

Theme: Intention, scope, and a clean manuscript

Day 1: Anchor Your Why + Reader.

- Write your Purpose Statement + Define your Dream Reader.

- Choose your daily writing window.

Day 2: Book Type & Outcome → Define book type and reader transformation.

Day 3: Structure Map → Outline chapters and signature stories.

Day 4: Gather and Organize → Combine your writing into one document.

Day 5: Rest & Reset → Step away to gain perspective.

Day 6: Read Like a Reader → Highlight strengths and confusion points.

Day 7: Cut Clutter, Keep Gold → Trim and tighten your first edit.

WEEK 2 — EDIT & POLISH (DAYS 8–14)

Theme: Refine your manuscript for publication.

Day 8: Line-Level Edit → Read aloud and smooth phrasing.

Day 9: Self-Edit Tools → Use Grammarly/Hemingway without losing your voice.

Day 10: Beta Readers → Recruit 3–5 readers for feedback.

Day 11: Integrate Feedback → Keep only what strengthens your message.

Day 12: Optional Professional Edit → Request a sample edit.

Day 13: Proof Pass → Check typos and details.

Day 14: Format Decision → Choose trim size and layout tool.

WEEK 3 — FORMAT, COVER, ISBN & PLATFORMS (DAYS 15–21)

Theme: Turn your manuscript into a book.

- Format interior and eBook.
- Add front & back matter.
- Create cover design and full-wrap PDF.
- Assign ISBN and barcode.
- Upload to KDP (+ optional IngramSpark).

WEEK 4 — PROOFS, PRE-LAUNCH & LAUNCH (DAYS 22–30)

Theme: Final checks and launch with intention.

- Review proof copies and update files.
- Optimize metadata and description.
- Build landing page + launch assets.
- Announce launch date and recruit review team.
- Record launch content (reel or podcast).
- Perform final tech checks.
- **Day 29:** Launch Ritual → Light a candle, breathe, and hit "Publish."
- **Day 30:** Sustain Momentum → Share reviews, pitch podcasts, plan 30-day content.

For extra guidance, revisit the chapters throughout *Write It Anyway* that align with each stage, or connect with me for 1:1 mentoring via carolinebakker.com.

You don't need permission.

You need a plan.

This is it.

EPILOGUE: WRITING AS A SOUL'S CALLING

RETURNING TO THE LIGHT WITHIN

Earlier this year, my dear soul sister Katja introduced me to the teachings of Kabbalah by David Ghiyam. I had explored many spiritual paths before — neuroscience, energetics, the Law of Attraction — but when I first listened to David Ghiyam speak about *Tikkun*, the concept of the soul's correction, something deep inside me stirred. It felt as though someone had finally put words to what my heart had always known.

I remember thinking, *This is so logical. It all makes sense.*

For years, I'd been learning about the soul's journey — through the teachings of Dolores Cannon and my own intuitive experiences. I had already come to understand that our souls choose their lessons before birth, that each challenge is sacred, and that we return to Earth to evolve through contrast and compassion. But Kabbalah gave me a language for it — not as abstract spirituality, but as divine structure. It showed me that life's struggles are not punishments, but invitations. They are the sacred curriculum of the soul.

That understanding changed how I saw everything — including writing.

Writing had always been part of my healing journey, but I began to see it as something greater: part of my *Tikkun*. My correction. My soul's purpose.

I realised that one of my lifelong patterns — and lessons — was learning to use my voice. To speak truth instead of staying silent. To be seen instead of hiding. To create light through words rather than hold my stories in shame. Each book I've written — *The Healing Journey*, *Thriving Naturally with ADHD*, *Return to the Heart*, and now *Write It Anyway* — has been a step in that sacred process. Every page, every sentence, a piece of my soul returning home.

That's also why I wrote my children's book, *I Chose You: A Soul's Journey to Earth*, released in August 2025. It was born from the same awareness — that we, as souls, choose our parents, our lessons, and our path before we arrive. I wanted my daughter, and all children, to grow up knowing that they are here on purpose. That even their challenges are part of their divine design.

Now I see that my role as a writer, teacher, and mother is also my role as a soul — to transform experiences into light, to turn wounds into wisdom, and to share that light with others. That is *Tikkun*. That is purpose.

If you are reading these words, perhaps writing is part of your soul's purpose too. Perhaps your story — the one you've been afraid to tell — is not just yours, but a vessel through which healing can flow to others.

When you write with awareness, you don't just create a book — you create energy. You send ripples of consciousness into the world. Your words become threads of light woven into the collective story of humanity.

So as you close this book and begin your own, I invite you to ask yourself:

What is my soul here to express?

What lesson am I meant to integrate and share?

What part of my Tikkun *does this book represent?*

May your writing become an act of remembrance — a way of returning to who you truly are.

May your story serve as a torch for others still walking through the dark.

And may every word you write carry the light of your soul's wisdom forward, long after this lifetime ends.

Because in the end, your book is more than pages bound together — it's a legacy of light.

A reflection of your soul's journey home.

THE HEALING AUTHOR'S MANIFESTO

I believe stories are medicine. Every time a woman writes her truth, she heals herself—and someone else she may never meet.

I believe words carry energy, and intention shapes impact. Creativity is not a luxury, but a lifeline.

Publishing is not about perfection, but permission — the permission to be seen, to be heard, to take up space in a world that once told us to shrink.

I believe in integration — where art meets healing, where structure meets spirit, where technology serves consciousness.

I believe that money can be holy, that integrity and abundance belong in the same sentence, and that we can thrive as we serve.

I believe in the ripple — that one healed voice awakens a thousand more. And I believe in you — in your story, your courage, your willingness to write it anyway.

Because when one of us writes, we all rise.

BONUS CHAPTER: HOW TO CREATE AND SELF-PUBLISH YOUR BOOK IN ONE DAY (EVEN IF YOU DON'T LIKE WRITING)

A COMPLETE STEP-BY-STEP GUIDE — FROM VOICE NOTE TO BOOK LAUNCH.

Y ou don't need to be a writer to become an author. You just need your voice, your story, and the right structure to bring it to life.

This is your shortcut to authorship — the heart of *Write It Anyway*.

In this chapter, I'll show you exactly how to create your book from scratch using tools you already have on your phone, how to title and structure it, how to design your cover, and how to publish it on Amazon so it's available worldwide — without hiring a publisher or paying thousands in fees.

By the end of this chapter, you'll have everything you need to go from voice note to published book.

STEP 1: SPEAK YOUR STORY (THE 3-PART VOICE NOTE METHOD)

Writing doesn't have to mean sitting in front of a laptop. You can literally *speak* your book into existence. All you need is your phone's voice recorder and about 45 minutes of uninterrupted space.

Record three short voice notes, one for each part of your story:

1. The Breakdown — What Happened

- Start with the truth.
  - What was happening in your life before things shifted?
  - What challenge, event, or emotion brought you here?
  - What patterns or beliefs kept you stuck?

Example: "I was exhausted, pretending everything was fine, but inside I was falling apart."

2. The Breakthrough — What Shifted

- Describe the turning point.
  - What realisation, person, or practice helped you heal or change?
  - What lessons began to unfold?
  - What new decisions did you make?

Example: "When I stopped trying to fix myself and started listening to my body, I found peace for the first time in years."

3. The Becoming — Who You Became

- End with the transformation.
  - Who are you now because of what you went through?
  - What wisdom or message do you want to pass on?
  - How do you want your reader to feel after reading your story?

Example: "Today, I live intentionally, creatively, and slowly. I don't chase — I create. And that shift changed everything."

Reflection Prompt:

What story are you ready to speak out loud — not to impress, but to express?

STEP 2: TRANSCRIBE YOUR VOICE NOTES

Upload your recordings to a transcription tool. These will turn your spoken story into written text automatically. **Popular tools:**

- Otter.ai — https://otter.ai
- Notta.ai — https://www.notta.ai
- Descript — https://www.descript.com
- Whisper by OpenAI — https://openai.com/research/whisper

Once transcribed, copy the text into a Word or Google Doc. Don't worry about grammar or structure yet — you'll refine later. What matters is that your story now exists *outside* of your head.

Tip: You can also play the voice note on your computer, and open Notes (on Apple) on your iPhone and then use the "dictation" option on your keyboard to dictate your own content (no external software needed).

STEP 3: STRUCTURE YOUR STORY

Now, organise your text using the same 3-part structure:

1. **The Breakdown** — Set the stage. What happened?
2. **The Breakthrough** — What shifted? What changed?
3. **The Becoming** — Who did you become, and what's your message?

Each story can become one **chapter** in your book. If you record several stories or lessons, you'll naturally create multiple chapters.

Tip: Aim for 6–10 chapters in your first book. Each chapter can be 1,000–2,000 words — easily achievable from short voice notes.

STEP 4: CRAFT YOUR BOOK TITLE AND SUBTITLE

Your title is a promise. It tells readers what your book will help them *feel, learn, or become.* Here's a simple formula: **[Emotional Outcome] + [Core Theme or Journey]**

Examples:

- *Write It Anyway: How to Turn Your Healing Story into a Self-Published Book That Helps Others*
- *The Healing Journey: Navigating Adult ADHD and PMDD*
- *Return to the Heart: A Journey to Heal Your Inner Child and Reclaim Your Power*

Then add a **subtitle** that tells readers exactly what they'll gain:

A Step-by-Step Guide to Healing, Writing, and Self-Publishing Your Story

Tips for choosing your title:

- Keep it between 3–6 words for memorability.
- Make it clear, not clever.
- Use emotional resonance over intellectual complexity.
- Test your title by saying it out loud — it should *feel* true.
- Once you have your title, use it as your *north star.* Everything else — your cover, your tone, your message — should align with it.

Tip: You can use AI to help you find the most suitable title and subtitle, and you can refer to appendix B for some useful prompts.

STEP 5: LET AI HELP YOU POLISH

Copy your raw transcript into ChatGPT (https://chat.openai.com) or your preferred AI platform, and use prompts like:

> *"Rewrite this transcript into a clear, engaging book chapter using my natural tone. Organize it into sections: The Breakdown, The Breakthrough, The Becoming."*

Or:

> *"Turn this personal story into a healing book chapter with lessons and reflection prompts at the end."*

You can also ask AI to:

- Suggest chapter titles
- Summarise your key message
- Format your manuscript for flow

Remember, *you are the creator.* AI simply helps you shape what's already within you. For more details on how to use AI see chapter 13 How to Use AI as a Creative Partner.

Tip: Refer to appendix B for more AI prompts to try.

STEP 6: FORMAT YOUR MANUSCRIPT

Once your chapters are refined, paste them into a clean Word or Google Doc. Add:

- A **title page** (Book title, author name, copyright year)
- **Table of Contents**
- **Dedication or Preface**
- Each chapter starting on a new page

You can format your book for print using **Reedsy Book Editor** (https://reedsy.com/write-a-book) or **Atticus** (https://atticus.io). Save your file as a **.docx** (for editing) and a **PDF** (for uploading later).

Tip: get your free book template from https://stan.store/ amazonwarrior/p/grab-your-free-6x9-book-template

STEP 7: DESIGN YOUR COVER

Your book cover is the first impression. You can design it yourself using **Canva Pro** or hire a freelancer via **Fiverr** (https://www.fiverr.com) or **Upwork** (https://www.upwork.com).

Canva template for book covers:

- https://www.canva.com/templates/book-covers/

Checklist for your cover:

- Include title, subtitle, and your author name.

- Match the tone of your book (soft for healing, bold for empowerment).
- Use clear fonts and high contrast colors.
- Ensure size fits your chosen publishing platform (KDP = 6x9 inches standard).

If you want to learn about choosing imagery, fonts, and visual tone, refer to **Chapter 14: Designing Your Cover with Intention** (pages 225–235).

STEP 8: GET YOUR ISBN

Every book needs an ISBN — the unique identifier that allows it to be sold in stores and online.

Options:

- **Amazon KDP (free)** will assign an ISBN automatically when you publish.
- **Bowker (paid)** lets you purchase your own ISBN if you want full ownership.
    - Website: https://www.myidentifiers.com
    - Cost: around USD $125 per ISBN (as of 2025).

If you plan to publish multiple books, it's worth owning your ISBNs.

STEP 9: SELF-PUBLISH YOUR BOOK

You can publish your book globally using **Amazon KDP (Kindle Direct Publishing)** — the most accessible and beginner-friendly platform.

1. Go to https://kdp.amazon.com
2. Create an account or log in with your Amazon details.
3. Click **"Create a New Title"** → **Paperback**
4. Fill out:
   - **Book Title**
   - **Subtitle**
   - **Author Name**
   - **Description (your book blurb)** → Example: "A practical, heartfelt guide to healing through writing and turning your story into a published book."

5. Add up to **7 keywords** to help readers find your book. → Example: self-publishing, healing, ADHD, PMDD, mindfulness, memoir, women's empowerment
6. Choose your **category** (e.g., Self-Help / Creativity / Memoir).
7. Upload your **manuscript (PDF)** and **cover file (PDF)**.
8. Set your **price** (USD $14.99–$24.99 is standard for paperbacks).
9. Review and click **"Publish."** Your book will appear on **Amazon within 24–72 hours**.

STEP 10: SHARE YOUR MESSAGE

Once your book is live:

- Share it on your social media.
- Add it to your email signature.
- Host a live reading or mini-workshop.

- Create a QR code linking directly to your Amazon page (use https://www.qr-code-generator.com).
- Celebrate! You're a published author.

STEP 11: EXAMPLE: CREATE YOUR BOOK IN A SINGLE DAY

- **Morning:** Record 3–5 voice notes.
- **Midday:** Transcribe with Otter.ai or Descript.
- **Afternoon:** Edit in ChatGPT using *The Breakdown → The Breakthrough → The Becoming.*
- **Evening:** Format and upload to KDP. By bedtime, you'll have your first book draft — or even a live publication.

STEP 12: OPTIONAL TOOLS & RESOURCES

- **Amazon KDP Help Pages:** https://kdp.amazon.com/help
- **Reedsy Book Title Generator:** https://blog.reedsy.com/book-title-generator/
- **Canva Book Cover Templates:** https://www.canva.com/templates/book-covers/
- **ISBN (Bowker):** https://www.myidentifiers.com
- **Self-Publishing School (Free Resources):** https://self-publishingschool.com
- **CarolineBakker.com Resources:** https://www.carolinebakker.com

FINAL REFLECTION

What's stopping you from speaking your story today? Your message doesn't need permission. It needs a microphone.

You don't need perfect grammar, fancy software, or a publishing deal. You need truth, structure, and action.

When you tell your story, you heal. When you publish it, you help others heal too. Your story is medicine.

Speak it. Write it. Publish it anyway.

APPENDIX A: LEGAL & ETHICAL ESSENTIALS

PROTECTING YOUR WORK, YOUR STORY, AND YOUR ENERGY

Publishing your story is an act of courage — and it also comes with a few practical responsibilities.

This section isn't meant to overwhelm you. Think of it as gentle guidance to help you share your truth safely, ethically, and with full creative sovereignty.

1. COPYRIGHT: YOUR WORDS, YOUR RIGHTS

The moment you write something, it's automatically protected by copyright. That means no one can legally reproduce, distribute, or adapt your work without permission.

You don't *need* to register your copyright to own it — but registration adds an extra layer of proof if disputes ever arise.

- **In the U.S.:** Register at copyright.gov.

- **In Australia:** Copyright is automatic and free; no registration needed.
- **In the U.K. & EU:** Same — automatic upon creation.

Tip: Always keep dated drafts or backups of your manuscript as evidence of authorship.

2. DISCLAIMERS FOR HEALING AND WELLNESS BOOKS

If your book touches on health, trauma, or emotional healing, include a short disclaimer — it protects both you and your readers.

Example:

This book is intended for educational and inspirational purposes only. It does not replace medical, psychological, or professional advice. Always consult qualified professionals regarding your personal health or wellbeing.

It doesn't dilute your message — it demonstrates integrity and professionalism.

3. PERMISSIONS AND PERSONAL STORIES

When sharing stories that involve real people:

- **Get consent in writing** if the story is identifiable.
- **Change names and details** to protect privacy.
- **Avoid defamation** — never portray someone as

harmful or negligent unless it's provably factual and relevant to your story's truth.

If the person has passed away, still approach with reverence. The energy of respect matters just as much as the legalities.

4. USING QUOTES, LYRICS, AND EXTERNAL CONTENT

Quoting a few lines from another author or public figure can enrich your book — but stay within **"fair use"** or **seek permission**.

- Short quotes (a few sentences) for commentary or review are usually fine.
- Song lyrics, poems, or large excerpts require permission.
- Always **credit the original creator** — it honors both ethics and energy.

5. PLAGIARISM AND AI ETHICS

If you use AI tools during writing or editing, make sure the words that remain are *yours*.

AI can assist — but authenticity must come from lived experience.

Include a note in your acknowledgments if you used AI for structure, summaries, or research. Transparency builds trust and models conscious creativity.

Remember: You are responsible for anything you publish under your name — even if it was "suggested" by a tool.

6. BUSINESS BASICS FOR INDEPENDENT AUTHORS

If you plan to sell books, courses, or related products:

- Keep records of sales and royalties for tax purposes.
- Consider a simple business setup — such as a sole trader, LLC, or company (depending on your country).
- Register your ISBNs under your own imprint (your publishing brand name) to retain full control.

This small step gives your work a professional foundation and signals to the world that you're not "just writing" — you're building a body of work.

7. ENERGY AND INTEGRITY

Legal protection matters — but so does energetic protection.

When you create with respect, transparency, and integrity, you set a frequency of trust.

Your readers will feel it.

Your book will carry it.

And your story will travel safely — exactly as it's meant to.

APPENDIX B: AI PROMPTS TO TRY

You don't need to be "techy" to use AI. You just need curiosity, clarity, and intention.

Think of prompts as conversation starters — gentle questions that help the technology understand what you're trying to create.

The clearer your energy and direction, the more aligned the response will be.

Here are a few powerful prompts to experiment with during your writing journey:

FOR STRUCTURE AND FLOW

Use these when your ideas feel scattered or you can't quite see the big picture yet.

- "Help me organize my book about [topic] into a clear, three-part journey from struggle to transformation."
- "Here are my rough notes. Can you group them into emotional or thematic stages that mirror the reader's healing process?"
- "Based on this draft, what would be a natural flow of chapters if I want the story to feel like a journey — not just information?"

Tip: Once AI suggests a structure, read it out loud. If it doesn't flow naturally when spoken, it won't feel authentic when read. Adjust until it matches your inner rhythm.

FOR SUMMARIES AND SIMPLIFICATION

When you've written a lot and need help distilling your message without losing its emotion or depth.

- "Summarize this section in one paragraph that keeps the emotional resonance but reads clearly."
- "Turn this 1,000-word draft into a 300-word version for a book proposal without losing its soul."
- "Rewrite this explanation so it sounds more human, warm, and conversational — as if I'm talking to a friend."

Tip: Always reread the AI output *in your voice*. Edit intuitively — your tone is your signature.

FOR RESEARCH AND SCIENCE INTEGRATION

Perfect for health, psychology, or personal development authors who blend storytelling with evidence.

- "Summarize three peer-reviewed studies on [topic] and explain them in simple, compassionate language."
- "Give me an overview of the latest research on [condition or concept], especially focusing on holistic or mind-body perspectives."
- "Find key statistics or findings that support the emotional benefits of writing therapy or mindfulness."

Tip: Always verify sources. Use AI for discovery, not as your final authority. Research becomes healing when you filter it through your own discernment.

FOR READER EXPERIENCE AND CONNECTION

When you want to make your book more interactive, reflective, and heartfelt.

- "Write five reflection questions based on this chapter's theme that invite gentle self-inquiry."
- "Suggest affirmations or journaling prompts that align with the emotional lesson of this chapter."
- "Create a short guided exercise that helps the reader embody what they've just learned."

Tip: Let AI help you brainstorm — but always test the prompts yourself. You'll know instantly which ones resonate and which ones feel hollow.

FOR MARKETING AND CLARITY

Because even soulful books need strategy.

Use these prompts to refine how you communicate your message to the world.

- "Write a 150-word book description that feels empowering, warm, and authentic to the tone of a healing memoir."
- "Summarize this book in one sentence that would connect deeply with women seeking transformation."
- "Write an author bio that sounds grounded, wise, and human — not corporate or salesy."

Tip: Once AI drafts your copy, speak it out loud. If it feels like *you* could have said it, keep it. If it sounds like a marketing robot, rewrite it with heart.

APPENDIX C: BIBLIOGRAPHY

Chapter 1 — Writing Your Story as a Healing Act

Pennebaker, James W., and Joshua M. Smyth. *Opening Up by Writing It Down: How Expressive Writing Improves Health and Eases Emotional Pain.* New York: Guilford Press, 2016.

Sloan, Denise M., and Brian P. Marx. "Taking Pen to Hand: Evaluating Theories Underlying the Written Disclosure Paradigm." *Clinical Psychology: Science and Practice* 11, no. 2 (2004): 121–137.

Kross, Ethan, and Jason Moser. "Why Expressive Writing Works: From Emotional Processing to Cognitive Reappraisal." *Current Directions in Psychological Science* 27, no. 2 (2018): 93–98.

Graham, Lauren. *Someday, Someday, Maybe.* New York: Ballantine Books, 2013.

Chapter 2 — Turning Pain into Power

Frankl, Viktor E. *Man's Search for Meaning.* Boston: Beacon Press, 2006.

Brown, Brené. *Rising Strong: The Reckoning. The Rumble. The Revolution.* New York: Random House, 2015.

Neff, Kristin. *Self-Compassion: The Proven Power of Being Kind to Yourself.* New York: William Morrow, 2011.

Siegel, Daniel J. *The Developing Mind: How Relationships and the Brain Interact to Shape Who We Are.* New York: Guilford Press, 2020.

Dispenza, Joe. *Breaking the Habit of Being Yourself: How to Lose Your Mind and Create a New One.* Carlsbad, CA: Hay House, 2012.

Chapter 3 — Your Story as Service

Goddard, Neville. *The Power of Awareness.* New York: TarcherPerigee, 1952.

Thich Nhat Hanh. *The Art of Communicating.* New York: HarperCollins, 2013.

Sinek, Simon. *Start with Why: How Great Leaders Inspire Everyone to Take Action.* New York: Portfolio, 2009.

Jung, Carl. *The Undiscovered Self.* Princeton, NJ: Princeton University Press, 1990.

Myss, Caroline. *Sacred Contracts: Awakening Your Divine Potential.* New York: Harmony Books, 2001.

Chapter 4 — What Kind of Book Are You Writing?

Lamott, Anne. *Bird by Bird: Some Instructions on Writing and Life*. New York: Anchor Books, 1994.

Pressfield, Steven. *The War of Art: Break Through the Blocks and Win Your Inner Creative Battles*. New York: Black Irish Entertainment, 2002.

Karr, Mary. *The Art of Memoir*. New York: Harper, 2015.

Didion, Joan. *The Year of Magical Thinking*. New York: Alfred A. Knopf, 2005.

Gornick, Vivian. *The Situation and the Story: The Art of Personal Narrative*. New York: Farrar, Straus and Giroux, 2001.

Chapter 5 — How to Start (Even When It's Messy)

Gilbert, Elizabeth. *Big Magic: Creative Living Beyond Fear*. New York: Riverhead Books, 2015.

Dweck, Carol S. *Mindset: The New Psychology of Success*. New York: Random House, 2006.

Clear, James. *Atomic Habits: An Easy & Proven Way to Build Good Habits & Break Bad Ones*. New York: Avery, 2018.

Amabile, Teresa M., and Steven J. Kramer. *The Progress Principle: Using Small Wins to Ignite Joy, Engagement, and Creativity at Work*. Boston: Harvard Business Review Press, 2011.

Chapter 6 — Writing Through the Body

Van der Kolk, Bessel A. *The Body Keeps the Score: Brain, Mind, and Body in the Healing of Trauma*. New York: Viking, 2014.

Levine, Peter A. *Waking the Tiger: Healing Trauma*. Berkeley, CA: North Atlantic Books, 1997.

Maté, Gabor. *When the Body Says No: Exploring the Stress-Disease Connection*. Toronto: Vintage Canada, 2003.

Marich, Jamie. *Trauma and the Twelve Steps: A Complete Guide to Enhancing Recovery*. Eau Claire, WI: PESI Publishing, 2020.

Sacks, Oliver. *Musicophilia: Tales of Music and the Brain*. New York: Alfred A. Knopf, 2007.

Chapter 7 — Writing Through the Mind

Kabat-Zinn, Jon. *Wherever You Go, There You Are: Mindfulness Meditation in Everyday Life*. New York: Hyperion, 1994.

Csikszentmihalyi, Mihaly. *Flow: The Psychology of Optimal Experience*. New York: Harper & Row, 1990.

Hanson, Rick. *Hardwiring Happiness: The New Brain Science of Contentment, Calm, and Confidence.* New York: Harmony Books, 2013.

Siegel, Daniel J. *Mindsight: The New Science of Personal Transformation.* New York: Bantam, 2010.

Chapter 8 — Writing in Sync with Your Cycle

Briden, Lara. *Period Repair Manual: Natural Treatment for Better Hormones and Better Periods.* Christchurch, NZ: Lara Briden Publishing, 2020.

Vitti, Alisa. *In the FLO: Unlock Your Hormonal Advantage and Revolutionize Your Life.* New York: HarperOne, 2020.

Gottfried, Sara. *The Hormone Cure.* New York: Scribner, 2013.

Resch, Elyse, and Evelyn Tribole. *Intuitive Eating: A Revolutionary Program That Works.* New York: St. Martin's Griffin, 2012.

Cabeca, Anna. *The Hormone Fix.* New York: Ballantine Books, 2019.

Chapter 9 — Writing for Longevity

Sapolsky, Robert M. *Why Zebras Don't Get Ulcers.* New York: Holt Paperbacks, 2004.

McEwen, Bruce S. *The End of Stress as We Know It.* Washington, DC: Joseph Henry Press, 2002.

Ratey, John J. *Spark: The Revolutionary New Science of Exercise and the Brain.* New York: Little, Brown and Company, 2008.

Walker, Matthew. *Why We Sleep: Unlocking the Power of Sleep and Dreams.* New York: Scribner, 2017.

Chapter 10 — From Scattered Pages to Soulful Chapters

Cron, Lisa. *Story Genius: How to Use Brain Science to Go Beyond Outlining and Write a Riveting Novel.* New York: Ten Speed Press, 2016.

Pinkola Estés, Clarissa. *Women Who Run With the Wolves: Myths and Stories of the Wild Woman Archetype.* New York: Ballantine Books, 1992.

Pressfield, Steven. *Turning Pro.* New York: Black Irish Entertainment, 2012.

Chapter 11 — The Emotional Work of Writing

Neff, Kristin. *Fierce Self-Compassion: How Women Can Harness Kindness to Speak Up, Claim Their Power, and Thrive.* New York: HarperOne, 2021.

Brown, Brené. *Daring Greatly: How the Courage to Be Vulnerable Transforms the Way We Live, Love, Parent, and Lead.* New York: Gotham Books, 2012.

Maté, Gabor, and Daniel Maté. *The Myth of Normal: Trauma, Illness, and Healing in a Toxic Culture.* New York: Avery, 2022.

Chapter 12 — Editing Made Simple
Clark, Roy Peter. *Writing Tools: 55 Essential Strategies for Every Writer.* New York: Little, Brown and Company, 2006.

King, Stephen. *On Writing: A Memoir of the Craft.* New York: Scribner, 2000.

Zinsser, William. *On Writing Well: The Classic Guide to Writing Nonfiction.* New York: Harper Perennial, 2016.

Gardner, John. *The Art of Fiction.* New York: Vintage, 1991.

Chapter 13 — How to Use AI as a Creative Partner
Roose, Kevin. *Futureproof: 9 Rules for Humans in the Age of Automation.* New York: Random House, 2021.

Kelly, Kevin. *The Inevitable: Understanding the 12 Technological Forces That Will Shape Our Future.* New York: Viking, 2016.

Amabile, Teresa M. *Creativity in Context.* Boulder, CO: Westview Press, 2012.

OpenAI. "GPT-4 Technical Report." *OpenAI Research Publications,* 2023.

Chapter 14 — Traditional vs. Self-Publishing
Penn, Joanna. *Successful Self-Publishing.* London: The Creative Penn, 2021.

Friedlander, Joel. *The Self-Publisher's Ultimate Resource Guide.* Marin, CA: Book Design Templates, 2020.

Baverstock, Alison. *How to Market Books.* London: Routledge, 2019.

Reid, Kristen. *The Business of Being a Writer.* Chicago: University of Chicago Press, 2018.

Chapter 15 — Becoming Your Own Publisher
IngramSpark. *IngramSpark Self-Publishing Guide.* LaVergne, TN: Ingram Content Group, 2024.

KDP (Kindle Direct Publishing). *KDP Help Center Documentation.* Amazon, 2024.

BookBub Partners. *Guide to Marketing Your Indie Book.* New York: BookBub, 2023.

Chapter 16 — Printing Your Proof

Friedlander, Joel. "Why You Should Always Order a Proof Copy Before Publishing." *The Book Designer*, 2020.

Print Ninja. *Book Printing Guide: Comparing Proofs and Materials*. Chicago: Print Ninja Publishing, 2022.

Chapter 17 — Format Options: eBook, Print, and Audio

Amazon KDP. *Formatting and Layout Guide for Kindle eBooks and Paperbacks*. Amazon, 2024.

ACX (Audiobook Creation Exchange). *Audiobook Production Guidelines*. Audible, 2024.

Reedsy. *How to Format a Book for Print and eBook*. London: Reedsy Learning, 2023.

Chapter 18 — Marketing Without Burning Out

Godin, Seth. *This Is Marketing: You Can't Be Seen Until You Learn to See*. New York: Portfolio, 2018.

Holiday, Ryan. *Perennial Seller: The Art of Making and Marketing Work That Lasts*. New York: Portfolio, 2017.

Pressfield, Steven. *Put Your Ass Where Your Heart Wants to Be*. New York: Black Irish Entertainment, 2022.

Chapter 19 — Building Your Author Brand

Sinek, Simon. *Find Your Why: A Practical Guide for Discovering Purpose for You and Your Team*. New York: Portfolio, 2017.

Miller, Donald. *Building a StoryBrand: Clarify Your Message So Customers Will Listen*. Nashville: HarperCollins Leadership, 2017.

Yohn, Denise Lee. *What Great Brands Do*. San Francisco: Jossey-Bass, 2014.

Chapter 20 — Staying Grounded Through Visibility

Nafousi, Roxie. *Manifest: 7 Steps to Living Your Best Life*. London: Michael Joseph, 2022.

Chopra, Deepak. *The Seven Spiritual Laws of Success*. San Rafael, CA: Amber-Allen Publishing, 1994.

Maté, Gabor. *Scattered Minds: The Origins and Healing of Attention Deficit Disorder*. Toronto: Vintage Canada, 2019.

Chapters 21–24 — Integration, Roadmap, and Living the Message

Means, Casey. *Good Energy*. New York: Penguin Press, 2024.

Bravington, Leah. *Soulful Productivity: A Modern Woman's Guide to Flow and Fulfillment.* London: Wild Grace Press, 2021.

Dispenza, Joe. *Becoming Supernatural: How Common People Are Doing the Uncommon.* Carlsbad, CA: Hay House, 2017.

Bakker, Caroline. *The Healing Journey: Navigating Adult ADHD and PMDD.* Dubai: Amazon Warrior Press, 2024.

———. *Healing on Empty: A Journey from Burnout to Radiant Energy.* Dubai: Amazon Warrior Press, 2025.

———. *Return to the Heart: A Journey to Heal Your Inner Child, Reclaim Your Power, and Awaken the Sacred Feminine.* Dubai: Amazon Warrior Press, 2025.

RESOURCES FOR HEALING AUTHORS

A COMPREHENSIVE GUIDE FOR WRITERS WHO ARE HEALING THROUGH THEIR WORDS AND READY TO SELF-PUBLISH WITH PURPOSE.

Writing is more than expression—it's transformation. It's where your healing, truth, and creative calling meet. This section is designed to support you on every level—body, mind, and spirit —as you bring your story into the world. Use what resonates. Return often. And remember: **your words are medicine.**

1. MIND-BODY SUPPORT FOR WRITERS

Nervous System & Energy Regulation

Writing about your truth can activate the nervous system. Keep your body grounded while you create.

Daily Practices:

- Breathwork: box breathing (4-4-4-4), alternate nostril breathing, or guided sessions with Soma Breath or Wim Hof.
- Grounding: walk barefoot, sit with your back against a tree, or use a grounding mat during writing sessions.
- Contrast therapy: sauna, cold showers, or cold plunges to reset your dopamine system and release tension.
- Acupuncture, massage, or restorative yoga to calm the body after deep writing sessions.

Nutritional & Supplement Support *(consult your practitioner)*

- Magnesium glycinate – relaxation and sleep
- Omega-3 fatty acids – focus and emotional regulation
- L-theanine or ashwagandha – calm alertness
- Rhodiola or ginseng – sustained energy
- Lion's Mane or reishi – clarity and focus

2. CREATIVE MINDSET AND FLOW

Journaling for Emotional Release

- *Morning Pages* (from *The Artist's Way* by Julia Cameron): three pages of stream-of-consciousness writing each morning.
- Stream-of-consciousness journaling: write without stopping, editing, or censoring.
- Prompts:
  - What truth am I afraid to write?
  - What memory still asks to be witnessed?
  - What would I say if I knew it could help someone heal?

Affirmations for Creative Courage

- My words are worthy, even when they are imperfect.
- I am not writing for approval, I am writing for alignment.
- My story matters because it is real.

Creative Flow Rituals

- Begin with intention: "May my words serve healing—for myself and others."
- End with gratitude and grounding: "Thank you for what came through me today."
- Move your body after emotional writing—walk, stretch, breathe, or rest.

Soundscapes for Writing

- Meditations by Amazon Warrior on Youtube "40Hz Gamma Waves for Writers Boost Focus, Creativity & Mental Clarity"
- Brain.fm – focus music based on neuroscience
- Endel – personalized sound environments for concentration
- Spotify playlists: "Deep Writing Flow," "528Hz Healing Frequency," "Focus Instrumental"

3. WRITING AND EDITING TOOLS

Writing Software

- Scrivener – for organizing manuscripts and research
- Google Docs – simple and accessible
- Notion or Obsidian – idea management and book structure
- Grammarly or ProWritingAid – grammar and clarity
- Hemingway App – readability check
- Descript – dictation and transcription

Organization Tools

- Trello or ClickUp – track your book progress
- Miro or MindMeister – visual mapping
- Freedom – block distractions while writing

4. SELF-PUBLISHING ESSENTIALS

Publishing Platforms

- IngramSpark – global print distribution
- Amazon KDP – eBook and print-on-demand
- Draft2Digital – distribute to Apple Books, Kobo, and Barnes & Noble
- BookVault – premium print and direct shipping

Technical Essentials

- Purchase ISBNs from your national agency: Bowker (US) or Nielsen (UK).
- Design covers using Canva Pro or BookBrush.
- Format interiors using Vellum or Atticus.
- Hire a qualified editor (developmental, line, and copy editing).
- Engage beta readers before your final draft.

Author Branding

- Build a website: Squarespace, Showit, or WordPress.
- Email marketing: ConvertKit or Flodesk.

- Create a professional press kit with your author bio, headshots, and book synopsis.

5. BUILDING YOUR AUTHOR PLATFORM

Content and Connection

- Use Instagram or YouTube to share writing insights, your story, and excerpts.
- Start a podcast using Spotify for Podcasters or Anchor.
- Write on Substack or Medium to share your voice and build readership.

Speaking and Visibility

- Attend author events and book festivals such as the Sharjah Children's Book Festival.
- Create a speaker one-sheet highlighting your topics and expertise.
- Use your book to launch workshops, retreats, or courses related to your message.

Visibility Tools

- BookBub – reader discovery and promotions
- Goodreads – author pages and community
- Linktree – simple link hub for your website and offers

6. HEALING THROUGH WRITING

Therapeutic Writing Techniques

- Write letters you never send—to your younger self, loved ones, or past experiences.
- Create a personal "timeline of transformation" listing your pivotal moments.
- Write dialogues with your body: ask, "What are you trying to tell me?"

Safety Practices

- Keep grounding items nearby: tea, candle, crystal, or music.
- Write in a calm space and close each session with a deep exhale.
- When emotional memories surface, pause and regulate your breath before continuing.

7. RECOMMENDED READING FOR HEALING AUTHORS

- *Big Magic* — Elizabeth Gilbert
- *The Artist's Way* — Julia Cameron
- *Writing Down the Bones* — Natalie Goldberg
- *Bird by Bird* — Anne Lamott
- *The War of Art* — Steven Pressfield
- *Writing as a Path to Awakening* — Albert Flynn DeSilver

- *Women Who Run With the Wolves* — Clarissa Pinkola Estés
- *When the Body Says No* — Dr. Gabor Maté
- *The Body Keeps the Score* — Bessel van der Kolk
- *Letters to a Young Poet* — Rainer Maria Rilke

8. COMMUNITIES AND CONTINUING SUPPORT

- Insight Timer Writer's Circle – mindfulness and creative community
  - https://insighttimer.com/
- Substack and Medium – share essays and stories
  - https://substack.com/
  - https://medium.com/
- Women Who Write International – writing and publishing network
  - https://www.womenwhowrite.org/
- Women Entrepreneur and Founders Helping Each Other Facebook Group - supportive network for women
  - https://www.facebook.com/groups/202402986297944)

9. MY RESOURCES FOR HEALING AUTHORS

Meditations by Amazon Warrior - Guided meditations for focus, calm, and creative restoration. Listen on:

- Insight Timer (Caroline Bakker)
  - https://insighttimer.com/amazonwarrior/guided-meditations
- Spotify (Meditations by Amazon Warrior)
  - https://open.spotify.com/show/05e4vr2WRSi82bnndoqMRs?si=f9b36c7ac89f47fa
- Apple Music (Meditations by Amazon Warrior)
- YouTube (Meditations by Amazon Warrior)
  - https://www.youtube.com/@meditationsbyamazonwarrior

Caroline's Courses on Insight Timer

- Mindfulness For Women With ADHD
- 5 Days Of Mindfulness
- Find them on https://insighttimer.com/amazonwarrior/guided-meditations

1:1 Coaching and Mentorship

Work directly with Caroline for personalised guidance in:

- Healing through storytelling.
- Nervous system support for creatives.
- Book development and self-publishing strategy.
- Health Coaching, DNA testing and more.

More information: www.carolinebakker.com

Speaking and Workshops

Caroline offers talks and workshops on creativity, holistic healing, and author empowerment.

For collaborations, interviews, or live events:

- https://www.carolinebakker.com/speaking-workshops-with-caroline-bakker/

Main Website and Newsletter

Stay connected for new meditations, workshops, and author tools: www.carolinebakker.com

10. WRITING PROMPTS FOR THE HEALING AUTHOR

1. What pain have I transformed into wisdom?
2. What story am I finally ready to release?
3. What lesson is my book trying to teach me first?
4. Who am I writing for, and how do I want them to feel?
5. What would it look like to write from love instead of fear?
6. What does my body need to feel safe before I write?
7. What truth in me feels tender but powerful?

ACKNOWLEDGMENTS

Writing this book has been one of the most liberating and healing experiences of my life. It's the culmination of late nights, quiet mornings, and the deep knowing that stories—especially the messy, imperfect ones—can become medicine when we choose to share them.

First and foremost, to my daughter, **Aria**, whose presence reminds me every day of what truly matters. You are my reason for showing up, for healing, and for continuing to create from a place of love and truth. You have been my greatest teacher in patience, surrender, and joy.

To my husband, **Shane**, thank you for your unwavering belief in me, even on the days when I doubted myself. Your love and grounding energy gave me the strength to keep writing when it felt impossible.

To my parents, **Aarnout and Inge**, thank you for giving me the roots to grow and the wings to explore. Your encouragement to follow my own path planted the seed for everything I've built today.

To **Chris, Hassan, Manar** and the team at **IngramSpark** and **Lightning Source**, thank you for seeing me, for giving me my first speaking opportunity at the **Sharjah Children's Festival in May 2025**, and for opening a door that changed the trajectory of my life. That panel was more than a milestone—it was a spiritual assignment. You gave me a platform to not only share my healing journey but to empower others to tell theirs.

To **Yasmen Ahmed**, author of *Lies That Shaped You*—my sister in soul and synchronicity—thank you for your friendship, your fire, and for placing *Big Magic* in my hands at exactly the right moment. Your encouragement breathed life into this book before I even knew it was forming.

To **Nick Santonastasso**, thank you for your mentorship and for creating *Stage Secrets*. Your course helped me clearly map the emotional and transformational journey of my reader—the same way you teach speakers to guide their audience. Using your worksheets, I defined each stage of transformation—from resistance to revelation—and wove that map into the heart of this book.

To my readers, students, and the **Meditations by Amazon Warrior** community—thank you for walking this path with me. Your messages and reflections remind me why this work matters and reaffirm that healing is something we do together.

And finally, to the woman I used to be—the one who thought she wasn't ready, wasn't qualified, wasn't enough—you were always the one. This book was written for you, and because of you. Thank you for not giving up.

With deep love and gratitude,

Caroline

ABOUT THE AUTHOR

Caroline Bakker is a meditation teacher, holistic health coach, and author dedicated to helping others heal naturally and reclaim their energy, focus, and emotional balance. With over 15 years of experience in wellness and fitness, she blends science, spirituality, and storytelling to empower women to transform their lives from the inside out.

Caroline is the creator of *Meditations by Amazon Warrior*, a global mindfulness brand with thousands of listeners on Spotify, Apple Music, and Insight Timer. Her work bridges neuroscience, nutrition, and nervous system regulation with the deeper art of self-compassion and inner healing.

Diagnosed with ADHD and PMDD in adulthood, Caroline turned her own challenges into her greatest teachers. Through her books—including *Thriving Naturally with ADHD*, *Healing on Empty*, and *Return to the Heart*—she shares the practical tools and lived wisdom that helped her move from burnout and imbalance to clarity, vitality, and purpose.

Born in the Netherlands and now based in Dubai, Caroline continues to write, teach, and guide others toward holistic healing, emotional freedom, and conscious living.

Learn more at **www.carolinebakker.com**.

ALSO BY CAROLINE BAKKER

The Healing Journey: Navigating Adult ADHD and PMDD - *Holistic Strategies and Practical Tips for Healing and Growth*

A deeply personal and science-backed exploration of ADHD and PMDD through the lens of holistic healing. Caroline shares her journey from overwhelm to empowerment, blending neuroscience, nutrition, and nervous system regulation to help readers transform struggle into strength.

Thriving Naturally with ADHD - *A Holistic Guide to Healing, Wellbeing, and Success*

A comprehensive guide to understanding and thriving with ADHD using a mind-body approach. Combining nutrition, lifestyle, mindfulness, and biohacking, Caroline offers practical tools to calm the nervous system, boost focus, and embrace neurodivergence as a superpower.

Return to the Heart - *A Journey to Heal Your Inner Child, Reclaim Your Power, and Awaken the Sacred Feminine*

A gentle yet powerful invitation to return to your true self. Through affirmations, reflection prompts, and emotional healing practices, Caroline guides readers in reconnecting with their inner child, softening old wounds, and awakening the sacred feminine within.

I Chose You - *A Soul's Journey to Earth*

A heartwarming children's story about love, purpose, and the soul's choice to be born. Told through poetic language and tender illustrations, it reminds parents and children alike that every soul arrives with divine intention—and that we are always exactly where we are meant to be.